The
BIG
Book of
ANGEL
TAROT

ALSO BY RADLEIGH VALENTINE

Books

Compendium of Magical Things

How to Be Your Own Genie

Card Decks

Angel Answers Oracle Cards

Angel Tarot Cards

Animal Tarot Cards

Archangel Power Tarot Cards

Fairy Tarot Cards

Guardian Angel Tarot Cards

All of the above are available online and
at your local bookstore. Please visit:

Radleigh's website: www.RadleighValentine.com
Hay House USA: www.hayhouse.com®
Hay House Australia: www.hayhouse.com.au
Hay House UK: www.hayhouse.co.uk
Hay House India: www.hayhouse.co.in

RADLEIGH VALENTINE

The
BIG
Book of
ANGEL
TAROT

The Essential Guide to Symbols, Spreads, and Accurate Readings

HAY HOUSE, INC.
Carlsbad, California • New York City
London • Sydney • New Delhi

Copyright © 2014 by Doreen Virtue and Radleigh Valentine
Revised Copyright © 2019 by Radleigh Valentine

Published in the United States by: Hay House, Inc.: www.hayhouse.com®
Published in Australia by: Hay House Australia Pty. Ltd.: www.hayhouse.com.au
Published in the United Kingdom by: Hay House UK, Ltd.: www.hayhouse.co.uk
Published in India by: Hay House Publishers India: www.hayhouse.co.in

Cover design: Tricia Breidenthal • *Interior design:* Riann Bender
Interior illustrations: Steve A. Roberts

This book was previously published in modified form as *The Big Book of Angel Tarot* by Doreen Virtue and Radleigh Valentine 978-1-4019-4370-7.

The Library of Congress has cataloged the earlier edition as follows:
Virtue, Doreen, date.
  The big book of angel tarot : the essential guide to symbols, spreads, and accurate readings / Doreen Virtue & Radleigh Valentine. -- 1st edition.
    pages cm
  ISBN 978-1-4019-4370-7 (tradepaper : alk. paper) 1. Tarot. 2. Angels--Miscellanea. I. Title.
  BF1879.T2V57 2014
  133.3'2424--dc23
                          2014010519

Tradepaper ISBN: 978-1-4019-5925-8
ebook ISBN: 978-1-4019-5926-5

10 9 8 7 6 5 4 3 2 1
1st edition, July 2014
Revised edition, September 2019

Printed in the United States of America

Certified Chain of Custody
SUSTAINABLE   Promoting Sustainable Forestry
FORESTRY
INITIATIVE   www.sfiprogram.org
             SFI-01268

SFI label applies to the text stock

To my beloved angel and tarot card community

CONTENTS

PART IV: Day-to-Day Life in the Minor Arcana

Minor Arcana

INTRODUCTION

The Creation of Angel Tarot

For decades, I have been fascinated with tarot. Long before I left my career in accounting to pursue a life as a spiritual teacher, I'd been using this ancient divinatory tool to get accurate and reliable answers for friends and clients. While to some, tarot and angels might have seemed like an odd combination, to me they went together like bread and butter! My first angel teacher, Carla, also loved tarot, so it felt completely natural to blend communication with angels and the wisdom of tarot to provide healing and insight to others.

While I loved tarot, I was also uncomfortable with the traditional imagery. I was on a never-ending quest for a set of cards that would match my vision of tarot as a compassionate and gentle way to communicate with the Divine. Sadly, this search only wound up filling my office with dozens of unused tarot decks. Many had varying positive aspects, but they also seemed to have distressing properties that made me set the decks aside. I found myself in readings with clients trying to minimize their ability to see the most challenging cards by keeping them turned toward myself or by rushing on to the next card in a spread. This was unfortunate because even the distressing cards in tarot have importance, so trying to ignore them was like ripping a chapter out of a book.

Then, magic happened! I had the opportunity to work with Hay House and my mentor to create my dream tarot deck. This became my first deck of angel tarot, aptly named *Angel Tarot Cards*—but it wouldn't be my last! I've been blessed to create multiple decks of angel tarot and oracle cards in the years since.

From the beginning, it was very important to me that the cards in my angel tarot decks not be some watered-down version of tarot. There's great depth and breadth in the human experience, and I want this concept to be fully represented in the cards. When I create a deck, I review all of the symbolism very carefully. When something distressing is removed from an image, I am diligent about replacing it with something peaceful that signifies the same thing. Card names are changed when necessary to more accurately convey the loving message embedded in even the most challenging cards.

Historically, tarot has been veiled in an air of mystery, but I don't understand what purpose there could possibly be in making messages from the Divine difficult to understand. So I add a few features to my angel tarot decks to help make them easier to use.

When I was initially learning the tarot as a young man, I'd taken a black marker and written the meaning on each card. As I learned, eventually I was able to replace that marked-up deck with clean cards. Inspired by this, I decided to place phrases and guidewords on each card so that my angel tarot decks could be used immediately out of the box without the need for study or research.

I believe that Source and the angels are always trying to guide us toward joy. Since tarot is merely a language for speaking to the Divine, every card in tarot is a message of love and is leading us to happiness. No matter what card you draw, it will *always* be love. It can't be anything *other* than love, because the Divine only wants you to be happy, and tarot is the Divine speaking to *you*.

While we're speaking about the Divine—or Source, the Universe, God, Goddess, or whatever name you like—as you read this book, keep in mind that I consider all of these to be just different words for the "all that is." If you use a different name, please just hear the word you most resonate with in your mind as you read.

My desire in creating angel tarot is to help you feel the love, compassion, and hope that tarot can bring into your life. I wanted to bring this centuries-old magical art out of the shadows and into the full view of Divine light!

Finally, it is my greatest desire that these cards will bring you immense blessings as you move along your spiritual path. I hope that you can now see tarot as it has always appeared to me: an angelic map leading the way to a joyous, magical life.

Love,
Radleigh

PART I

The BASICS of ANGEL TAROT

CHAPTER ONE

BRIGHT *and* BEAUTIFUL GUIDANCE

Tarot is a language of the Divine. It is one of the countless ways in which Heaven lovingly speaks to us in order to guide us on the path to joy. However, for centuries, this beautiful divination tool has been shrouded in secrecy and fear. By creating the *Angel Tarot Cards* (and writing this book), it is my intention to remove any anxiety by fully revealing this beautiful oracle and putting any concerns to rest.

Even tarot's beginnings seem mysterious. People have been led to believe for hundreds of years that tarot originated in ancient civilizations and was purposely encoded with secrets that only a chosen few were meant to understand. This concept has often created distress for sensitive people—not to mention the lack of confidence so many experience when even approaching a tarot deck.

Well, it's time to breathe a sigh of relief, because tarot was created for *all* of us! Its origins aren't in a dark chamber of an ancient secret society. No, it began as a creation of happiness, laughter, and togetherness—actually, as a game meant for families to play!

Now that may come as a surprise, but consider the energy that was placed into these cards from the very beginning: it was joy, creativity, and fun. And just like tarot, our lives are meant to be playful—a happy game that can bring us enlightenment and inspiration.

As time went by, tarot was appreciated by millions of people who enjoyed the game that it was created to be, but who were also seeking insight and guidance. They began to see something in the cards—a story that mirrored their lives. So tarot started to evolve. People shared their cards and their divinatory qualities with their friends and handed down the knowledge to their children and grandchildren.

Somewhere down the line, though, associations formed around tarot and other mystical arts that were perhaps created by well-meaning people. However, these individuals were most likely secretive types who enjoyed knowing things that others didn't. Sadly, their actions and possessive attitudes toward tarot made it seem intimidating, shadowy, and somewhat frightening. It was like taking a big blanket and throwing it over a very bright lantern.

Well, guess what? We're now in the 21st century, and we in the angel community don't like secret knowledge, exclusive societies, or intimidation. So the blanket has been lifted, and the lantern is shining brighter than ever!

~

Some ask what makes tarot work. Well, the answer to that question is simpler than one might think. Imagine people walking through an untamed forest. These explorers tell of their positive experiences to friends, who then want to see for themselves. Eventually the path through the forest gets worn down.

These are the trailblazers—much like the people who first saw epiphanies hidden in a card game. And since that time, millions have followed that path. Through the power of their combined belief and faith in tarot, they created a direct form of communication with Heaven. That's what tarot is!

What makes tarot work is all of us collectively seeking answers through a beautiful, loving divinatory tool. Most people use tarot to help *others* receive Divine guidance—and these individuals are Earth Angels in service to humankind.

So as you can see, tarot is still doing exactly what it was originally created to do—make people happy!

CHAPTER TWO

The BEGINNINGS *of* ANGEL TAROT

The history of tarot is fairly complex, with many twists and turns, according to historians. However, if we maintain a high-level overview, it can be explained rather easily.

The Origins of Tarot

The earliest evidence of tarot cards that we can find takes us to the early 15th century in northern Italy. Ordinary playing cards preexist tarot, but the adding in of the "fifth suit" of cards is traced back to the year 1420 or so. These cards are the predecessors of what we call the Major Arcana today. They were intended to be a set of trump cards to be played with a regular deck of 56 playing cards in a game called Tarrochi, which is still played today and is very much like Bridge.

Northern Italy was a manufacturing mecca for the creation of these types of cards. However, the number of trump cards varied by manufacturer, as did the order of the cards. They were often unnumbered and unnamed, so our understanding of the order that some decks were created in is often vague. Incidentally, The Fool card was often treated not so much as a trump card but as a sort of wild card in these decks.

We're blessed to have some very famous examples of these ancient decks because the very wealthy would commission artists to hand-paint the cards for them. These decks were considered works of art that were cared for and passed down through generations. Decks that were created via the printing press have rarely survived, and there are few examples of those cards.

Italians loved their tarot cards, and the business of creating them was robust! Tarot then spread to France when that country seized control of Milan in 1499. Within 20 years, Marseilles had become the center of tarot manufacturing in France. Slowly, not only did the cards get their numbering and naming conventions, but the order of the cards and the construction of the Major Arcana had largely become consistent. So, too, had most of the symbolism in the cards.

Tarot as a Divinatory Tool

There's evidence that ordinary playing cards were used for divinatory purposes earlier than the existence of tarot. This leads us to believe that tarot could have been used as a divination tool from its beginnings, in addition to being a playing-card game.

In the late 18th and early 19th centuries, alternative forms of spirituality became all the rage in France. Stories of tarot originating in ancient Egypt and then being brought to Europe by gypsies were spread in the streets, even though there's no evidence that this is true. Men who claimed to be able to read ancient Egyptian identified and attributed secret messages to the tarot, which were later found to be completely false by those who could decipher the language.

It's also important to note that there was no paper in ancient Egypt. When this was pointed out to those who were spreading the stories, they then claimed that the images were printed in Egypt on gold or other precious surfaces. Again, no evidence of this has ever been found. Still, these stories captured the public's imagination and led to the sense of secrecy and mystery surrounding tarot.

In the late 19th century, some secret societies claimed tarot as part of their teachings, using them in initiation ceremonies and in the training of their members. This further compounded the sense of fear and suspicion around tarot. It wasn't the cards themselves creating this fear; it was the people who were using them! Astrology, numerology, and other mystical arts were linked to individual cards in the tarot by these groups.

Two members of a secret society worked together to create a famous deck called the *Rider-Waite Tarot*. Arthur Edward Waite partnered with artist Pamela Coleman Smith to create this groundbreaking deck. (The word *Rider* referred to the publishing company of the deck at that time.)

Overflowing with symbolism and hidden meanings, this deck came out in 1909 and was heavily influenced by the Marseilles decks of France. The images were often tragic, if not outright frightening, and also difficult to understand.

It was at this time that Waite did the unconventional and flipped the positions of the Justice card and the Strength card in his deck, a departure from the way they'd been for centuries. He did this to line up the cards astrologically in a manner that he preferred. Incidentally, many tarotists today refer to this deck as the Waite-Smith deck in order to give credit to the artist for her part in its creation.

Alternative spirituality was also on the wane at this time, so tarot wasn't moving around in the circles of greater society. When people did see the cards, it was at a county fair being displayed at the booth of a fortune teller. The mystery and fear surrounding tarot was further compounded by the development of the movie industry. Tarot cards were never seen being used by average people seeking enlightenment, but rather were featured as tools of unscrupulous mediums who frightened those seeking advice by revealing fear-provoking images.

Time for a Change

As the decades marched on, many new interpretations of tarot were created. However, most of these decks followed the Rider-Waite deck very closely; the imagery and wording rarely changed. These new decks largely provided a new artist's interpretation, or were novelty decks reflecting a theme such as the Victorian Age or perhaps the story of King Arthur. By the year 2000, the options were endless. And yet, many of these decks were even more frightening and distressing than the centuries-old ones!

Many sensitive people were fascinated by tarot and wished to take advantage of this amazing tool, but their searches through the shelves of metaphysical bookstores left them feeling that there was just too much fear displayed on the cards.

As I discussed in the introduction of this book, I had the amazing opportunity to work with Hay House and artist Steve A. Roberts to create my first tarot deck, *Angel Tarot Cards*. Together, we diligently removed frightening words and images and replaced them with vocabulary and artwork that were positive yet retained the depth and accuracy of tarot.

After all, the cards are truth-tellers, but always in a kind and loving way. They were never meant to be frightening! After centuries of secrecy and darkness, tarot has been brought back out into the light where anyone can use the cards to get answers and guidance from Heaven and the angels.

CHAPTER THREE

The LANGUAGE
of ANGEL TAROT

Let's define some of the terms commonly used in the world of tarot. Understanding this vocabulary will make learning how to provide accurate readings easier and more comfortable.

Arcana

Arcana means "mysteries," referring not to secrets, but to the miraculously mysterious way that the Universe weaves itself through our lives. Tarot is broken into two primary sections called the **Major Arcana** and the **Minor Arcana.** The Major Arcana documents big, dramatic life events; while the Minor Arcana focuses on day-to-day life. So, loosely translated, you can think of them as the big mysteries and the little mysteries of life. (The plural of *arcanum* is *arcana*.)

Court Cards

The court cards refer to the Page, Knight, Queen, and King found in each of the suits of the Minor Arcana. They can represent people or situations in our lives (see Chapter 5).

The Dreamer's Journey

This is a story line that follows the 22 cards of the Major Arcana (see Chapter 4). The Dreamer is you and your dreams, or whoever is receiving the reading.

Duality Cards

Duality cards are those that can be interpreted as one extreme of a concept or the other, depending on the reading. For example, the Unity card may mean the need to take the traditional route when making a decision, or it can mean thinking outside the box. The Four of Earth may be cautioning people that they're spending too much money, or it may reflect a desire to lighten up and spend more (after all, you can't take it with you!). The message of a duality card depends on the other cards in the reading or an individual's particular situation.

Jumping Cards

Cards that seem to jump from the deck during shuffling or removal from the box are called "jumping cards." They're considered part of the reading and should be laid aside for reference once the other cards have been reviewed (see Chapter 8).

Pip Cards

This term refers to the cards numbered Ace to Ten in the suits of the Minor Arcana. The term means "a countable item," and refers back to a time when there were no pretty pictures on the Minor Arcana cards; there were only numbers and symbols (see Chapter 5).

Querent

This is a very common term in the tarot community that refers to the person who's getting the reading. When you do a reading for yourself, *you* are the querent. If you're providing insight through the cards for someone else, *that* person is the querent. In this book, I tend to refer to the querent as "the client."

Reversed Cards

Cards that come out of the deck upside down are called "reversed cards." Many tarot decks have different meanings for these cards. However in the *Angel Tarot Cards,* no additional meaning has been attributed. All you have to do is simply turn the card right-side up and proceed with the reading.

Significator

When a card reminds us of someone we know, this card is called a "significator." For example, someone might decide that the Queen of Wands has many of the traits of a sister, or that the image on the Knight of Air bears a striking resemblance to a nephew. This card may then come to represent those people in readings in the future, but only if it makes sense for those individuals to be showing up during that reading. It's not necessary to try to force these associations into readings even if a significator has been established.

Spreads

Spreads are guidelines for laying out cards for certain types of readings. Usually they have a specific pattern and meaning associated with each card, and are designed for particular topics such as romance, health, or life purpose. (See Chapters 9 and 10.)

CHAPTER FOUR

The DREAMER'S JOURNEY

The Major Arcana comprises the first 22 cards of tarot, numbered 0 to 21. These cards often symbolize major life events or other significant situations we're experiencing. For those who read cards for themselves or regular clients on a frequent basis, the impact of a Major Arcana card in a reading may be diminished (we can't have big life situations every day!). However, when the reading is for a stranger or an infrequent client, the Major Arcana signals important life events.

The Major Arcana can also reflect different times throughout our lives, including periods of births, marriages, careers, and spiritual growth. This is called "The Dreamer's Journey," and it can be very helpful as a way of understanding where clients are in their lives. Keep in mind that this can be literal or metaphorical. For example, The Empress card is about creativity and can therefore indicate pregnancy. Someone who draws this card in a reading may be about to have a baby, or may be concerned about "giving birth" to a cherished dream.

In The Dreamer's Journey, The Dreamer is the person receiving the reading. So if you're giving a reading to yourself, *you* are

The Dreamer. If you're giving a reading to someone else, that person is The Dreamer. As we go through each card in the journey, I'll be referring to The Dreamer as *you*.

The term *Dreamer* has many meanings, so let's define it. In the *Angel Tarot Cards,* The Dreamer refers to a person who has dreams and intentions—someone who's experiencing life as if in a sleeping dream. But being a Dreamer does *not* imply that you're merely dreaming about your goals. It's a positive term, meaning that *you* are important, and so too are your dreams. The *Angel Tarot Cards* will give you guidance on how to make your dreams come true.

It's also *very important* to keep in mind that while the youth on The Dreamer card is depicted as male, the story applies equally to both male and female personal journeys.

To help you understand this aspect of the tarot—and your own Dreamer's Journey—we're now embarking on a magical journey through the Major Arcana!

The Dreamer's Journey

0 – *The Dreamer:* This is the beginning. As The Dreamer, you have made the decision to take a leap of faith and embark on a new experience. Think of this card metaphorically—like being a newborn soul on Earth. You have arrived with optimism, excitement, and total faith that this adventure will be a grand success. You walk in complete faith.

1 – *The Magician:* Now that you (The Dreamer) have arrived, the first person you encounter is The Magician. From this magical being, you discover that you can manipulate the four elements in this world. You can make Fire and put it out with Water; you can breathe Air and till the Earth. You also have the ability to manage spiritual energy as well as earthly matter to create what you desire.

2 – *The High Priestess:* Understanding that you can create what you desire isn't the same thing as knowing what you *want* to create! So as The Dreamer you move on to learn from The High Priestess

about the importance of going within. You learn about meditation and listening to the voice of God, the angels, and your higher self. You ask the question: "Who am I, and what am I here to do?" A search for the discovery of your Divine life purpose has begun.

3 – *The Empress:* Your time as The Dreamer with The High Priestess was successful, and you now know what you want to do with your life. The Empress is a woman of amazing creative abilities; there's nothing she can't do once she puts her mind to it. So you learn from The Empress how to get things done—to put action behind your desires so that they can manifest in the real world.

4 – *The Emperor:* Creativity is a wonderful thing, but action without logic and organization can lead to chaos. The Emperor teaches every Dreamer he encounters the wisdom behind discipline and order, but The Emperor isn't without feeling. His work is generally for the greater good and seeing that people's needs are met. He just adds structure around creativity so that it can be as effective as possible.

5 – *Unity:* Discipline and order without morality can turn into tyranny. So the next stop on The Dreamer's Journey is the Unity card. Here, you realize that you want to be understood and accepted by a community of people; you also learn to be accepting of other people's points of view.

6 – *The Lovers:* Just like all Dreamers, as you grow up it's inevitable that you will eventually find love. This card is about life-changing love relationships. You come to understand the power of emotion and the beauty it can bring into your life. You also learn the importance of making choices from the heart and not always from the mind.

7 – *The Chariot:* The choices that you (as The Dreamer) have made follow you into adulthood, where you begin to be your own person. Through the use of sheer willpower and determination,

you'll be able to achieve great things and become a success in the world. You're young and strong and ready for life.

8 – *Justice:* As you leave home and venture out into the world, you must learn that there are consequences to your actions. You will come to understand that "the good you do comes back to you," and likewise, "What goes around, comes around." It will be important for you as The Dreamer to understand that you must stand up for what you know is right, or live with the results of your inaction. This card pushes the sensitive Dreamer to be assertive.

9 – *The Hermit:* Over time, you start to ask yourself some very powerful questions. You begin to seek meaning in the world, and your place within it. You set out on a quest for self-discovery that will define who you are going forward. As part of The Dreamer's Journey, you may seek solitude, or a mentor who can teach you about the deeper meaning of life.

10 – *The Wheel:* After time spent with The Hermit, you realize that you're starting to see how the world really works. You've gotten some of the answers that you're seeking, and now it's time to get moving again. The Dreamer *does* have a destiny, but it is one of your own creation. The Wheel represents the world in movement, particularly after a time of inaction.

11 – *Strength:* As you have evolved on The Dreamer's Journey, you've discovered the power of compassion and kindness. You've come to realize that forcing your will upon others doesn't lead to happiness. You've developed inner strength, and the knowledge that by moving along your path with courage tempered by gentleness, you experience more joy.

12 – *Awakening:* As all Dreamers do, you eventually come to a time in your life when things are stalled. Life feels a bit upside down, and your perceptions are forever changed by your experiences. You feel called upon to put your own needs aside in order to be of service to others. You realize that it feels good to let go . . . and let God be in control.

13 – *Release:* Recent experiences have given you clarity as to what really matters to you. You've also become aware that there are situations and people whose presence in your life are no longer conducive to your Divine life purpose. As the Dreamer, you embrace the endings that are necessary for you to grow in order to generate the new beginnings you desire. Your transition is a spiritual one.

14 – *Balance:* As The Dreamer, you've experienced a great deal along your path through the Major Arcana. It's now necessary to balance all those adventures and assimilate them into a single, cohesive philosophy of life. You've discovered that living a balanced life full of moderation and cooperation with others provides good health and contentment.

15 – *Ego:* As you continue to pursue your own development, you become aware of the impact of the ego upon your daily life. You've come to realize that by understanding your own inner challenges more deeply, you will be able to confront those aspects of yourself and regain your power over them. You now see that your belief that others can block your life path is an illusion. You wish to let go of worldly things that would tempt you away from a spiritual life.

16 – *Life Experience:* The time has come to break free of any remaining aspects of The Dreamer's world that hold you back from true happiness. Heaven, and your angels, will find a way of bringing true change and evolution into your life. Or you could choose to make those changes on your own and therefore feel more in control of the transition. But one way or another, you *will* be freed!

17 – *The Star:* You are now free of the hopelessness that once held you hostage. Your faith has become strong and unbreakable—so much so that water is allowed to be poured from the urns in an endless flow without any worry that they'll run out. The limitless abundance of the Universe is now completely clear to you. You have the faith to move mountains!

18 – *The Moon:* In your Dreamer's state of joy and hope, you aren't fully aware of the events that are going on around you. Your heightened intuitiveness tells you that there's more here than meets the eye, but you aren't sure what that means. So as not to be thrown off your path by fear and worry, you must cast aside the last of your insecurities and trust that the feelings you're experiencing will lead you out of the nighttime and into the morning.

19 – *The Sun:* The morning has come, and with it, the bright rays of enlightenment fill your soul! You feel nothing but joy and pride in your accomplishments along this journey. You're filled with self-confidence and an understanding that you can do anything with your life that you choose to and be a success. You have been reborn!

20 – *Renewal:* Now that you have successfully made your way to the last steps of the journey, you find yourself in a time of assessment and evaluation. The task before you is to seek out any unresolved issues within your heart and offer up forgiveness to any and all who desire it. So what will you do with your life now that you have so successfully defeated your ego and brought faith, hope, and confidence into your heart? Review all of your options carefully with a knowing in your soul that you will be successful at anything you attempt.

21 – *The World:* The journey is now complete! All of The Dreamer's plans have been fulfilled; and you are strong, whole, and radiant in your success. You have the option of pausing for a time or returning to the beginning of the journey to try something new. But for now, you get to bask in the perfection of the Divine.

CHAPTER FIVE

The MINOR ARCANA

The Minor Arcana cards reflect aspects of our daily lives such as our jobs, families, and financial situations. Although big life events are usually in the Major Arcana cards, significant experiences can also appear in the Minor Arcana. For example, there are cards in the Minor Arcana that reflect getting married, having a child, switching careers, and inheriting a significant sum of money. It's just that the majority of the Minor Arcana is about our desire to seek out a happy daily life.

There are four suits in the Minor Arcana that include ten pip cards and four court cards. As mentioned, the word *pip* means "a countable item." It's an old reference to the Ace through Ten cards, coming from a time when there were no images on those cards. Tarot cards were like ordinary playing cards with only symbols such as diamonds or clubs on them.

The four suits of the *Angel Tarot Cards* are *Fire, Water, Air,* and *Earth*—otherwise known as "the four elements." To attribute an element to each suit isn't a concept new to tarot. The suits in traditional tarot are Wands, Cups, Swords, and Coins, which have long been associated with each of those same elements, respectively.

The Suits

Fire: The suit of Fire represents the aspects of our lives where we feel great passion and excitement. In traditional tarot, this was the Wands suit. The Fire suit focuses on our creativity and passions. It's typical to see Fire cards in readings that relate to our careers; our desire to chase after beloved dreams; and artistic endeavors such as painting, acting, or writing. The ideas in the Fire suit can be full of adventure, or they may indicate a temporary pause in the action. But we're never really idle in the Fire suit. Even when we're not physically working on something, the Fire suit asks us to plan for the future. Fire can also represent any of our passions. For example, if clients have a passion for dogs, then a question in a reading regarding their pets may appear in cards of the Fire suit.

Water: For the emotional aspects of our world, we have the suit of Water. In traditional tarot, this was the Cups suit. The Water suit represents the deeper parts of our lives—for example, falling in love, having children, or making new friends with whom we feel deep intimacy. Our families, homes, and childhood memories are also within these cards. They can indicate the times when we celebrate getting engaged and married, and doing the hard work necessary to have a happy family life. The suit of Water also represents our spirituality and intuitive gifts.

Air: The suit of Air represents our intellect. In traditional tarot, this is the Swords suit. The Air cards focus on dazzling new ideas, inspired choices, and an ability to communicate that can bring a crowd to its feet. Yet the Air suit also describes the moments when we're unable to make a choice, find ourselves in conflict with others, or feel trapped by our own negativity. This is the suit of the mind, so we may experience fear or worry in the suit of Air. When such cards are displayed, it's our strong belief that tarot is trying to help us or our clients see that these moments are illusions from which we can awaken. At the very least, problems are creations of our own hands and therefore can be addressed. The suit of Air also represents legal concerns such as truth and justice.

Earth: Finally, we have the suit of Earth. In traditional tarot, this is the suit of Coins. The Earth cards focus on making money, paying our bills, and meeting our family's material needs. In this suit, we find our daily activities, jobs, and the search for financial security. While the other three suits often speak to matters that come from within (passion, emotion, and ideas), the suit of Earth is all about what's outside of us. Society, community, and our physical health are represented by these cards. The suit of Earth is also very concerned about the environment and how we care for our beautiful planet.

Each suit can be associated with a season of the year. However, there's debate in the card-reading community about which suit matches up to which season. The consensus seems to be that Fire = spring, Water = summer, Air = winter, and Earth = autumn. These associations also match the *Angel Tarot Cards.*

During a reading, it can be very telling to see if there's a lot of one particular suit in a spread, or if there's a suit missing. For example, if someone asks a question regarding a romantic relationship, we would hope to see cards from the suit of Water (love and emotion) and/or from the suit of Fire (passion and excitement). If these cards are missing from the reading, it prompts the question: "Where is the *feeling* in this relationship?"

A large number of Air cards (intellect and analysis) might indicate that one or both of the parties in the relationship aren't emotionally available, or see relationships intellectually rather than emotionally. A high number of Earth cards (finances and career) might indicate that someone is considering the relationship for financial security rather than the more nurturing aspects it could provide.

The Pip Cards

The pip cards are those numbered Ace through Ten in the four suits of the Minor Arcana. And numerically, these cards can have a common thread. For example, if a spread shows many cards that are numbered Five, which means "change" in both numerology and traditional tarot, then we can be assured that great change is coming for the recipient of the reading. However, let's talk about each of the numbers individually.

ACE CARDS

Aces indicate new beginnings or opportunities for a fresh start. They generally bring with them some type of energy for a new endeavor. This may include material gifts such as money, emotion, ideas, assistance from others, or a heightened excitement on the part of the client as to what's in store. Aces are often tied to the Page in the court cards, as both can indicate new information. Multiple Aces in a reading indicate someone who's opening up to a whole new phase touching on many different facets of life.

TWO CARDS

Twos often indicate friendships, romantic relationships, or any type of partnership between two or more people. The type of relationship indicated is generally portrayed by the suit. The Two of Fire is often a career-based relationship, while the Two of Water has more of a personal nature. Twos can also indicate the need to make the choice between two different options, as is reflected in the Two of Air and the Two of Earth. The energy of this number asks us to seek balance, harmony, and cooperation. It can also indicate duality in a situation, which implies multiple meanings at once. Multiple Twos in a reading can reveal the need to make choices on various fronts of one's life, as well as the need to work with others on various goals.

THREE CARDS

Threes represent creativity, growth, and self-expression. Three means two parents or a male and female energy giving birth to a new person or project. Three cards indicate a need to see clearly where we're headed and to make decisions based upon those goals. The concept of creativity in the Three cards extends to the birth of children in the Three of Water. The Three of Air tends to reflect the challenges that growth can bring into our lives when we feel unable to embrace change. A lot of Threes in a reading gives us insight that our clients are seeking expansion in many aspects of their lives. There's a strong need to create, and to grow into a stronger person.

Four Cards

Fours represent a solid foundation. Consider a table with four legs. It feels solid, stable, and secure. Fours also represent structure, order, balance, and discipline. Fours are the results of our efforts (or lack thereof). A large number of Fours in a reading indicates a moment of reflection. This may take the form of celebration, like the Four of Fire; or a need to reflect inwardly, like the Four of Air. It's often that reflection that leads to the change that comes about with the Fives.

Five Cards

Fives are often challenges that bring about opportunities. As mentioned earlier, this is the number of great change. With Fives, we learn to adapt—we spread our wings and break free of circumstances that no longer feel right to us. Oftentimes, Fives can show us a resistance to change. Human beings usually don't enjoy the uncertainty of change, so clients may be openly rebelling against the forward momentum that Heaven has in mind for them. However, Fives can also lead to freedom. Hindsight is 20/20, and once we're past the uncomfortable feelings of change, we often find that we're glad we went through it. Several Fives in a reading should be a heads-up that clients are experiencing changes in many areas of their lives. Reassure them that all will work out, while also having compassion for any fear they may be experiencing.

SIX CARDS

Sixes bring about harmony. After the uncertainty of the Fives, we're ready for a rest, which can range from elation due to a job well done, like the Six of Fire; to just plain relief over being finished with a challenge, like the Six of Air. Sixes indicate the resolution of past challenges that may bring about contentment or even joy. Sixes often generate a desire to reflect upon the past. Objectivity is important when looking backward so that we neither romanticize how things used to be, nor see them as worse than they were. A lot of Sixes in a reading should bring a smile to a client's face!

SEVEN CARDS

Sevens often bring with them a lot of soul-searching. There can be a longing for more out of life when Sevens are present. In assessing our progress, we may find ourselves lacking, and it can be easy to be unkind to ourselves, generating a need for self-forgiveness. Sevens indicate review, patience, and introspection. We wish to fully understand the truth of our situation and to gain clarity regarding the purpose of our lives. Spiritual development becomes a significant concern. Multiple Sevens in a reading indicate a pause in the action while we make choices regarding what we want to do next. Cards like the Seven of Fire or the Seven of Earth usually reflect a renewed determination to stay the course, while the Seven of Air and the Seven of Water can indicate uncertainty or difficulty in choosing our next steps. The specific Sevens in a reading give us an understanding of whether the client is moving along a path toward happiness, or standing still in procrastination.

EIGHT CARDS

Eights are an indicator of great progress and activity in our lives. They tell us that accomplishment through concerted effort is possible as long as we retain a positive mind-set. Eight is a number of great power, and therefore represents self-fulfilling prophecies. Optimistic hopes for ourselves are rewarded with the success we seek, while giving in to fear is likely to manifest that which we're most afraid of. Oftentimes when we have a lot going on in our lives, it can feel stressful. However, stress can sometimes stem from a great number of positive things, as the Eight of Fire tends to indicate. The Eight of Water and the Eight of Earth show our determination to make life better for ourselves. Several Eights in a reading will reflect those with a lot going on in their lives.

NINE CARDS

Nines often reflect extremes in optimism and pessimism. The positive is accentuated, but so is the negative. We may find ourselves attaining our goals in a spectacular fashion, or allow our fears to bring us to a grinding halt. Nines indicate that we've come a long way on our path. We may have paid what feels like a high price and feel the need to protect what we've created, as in the Nine of Fire. Or we may know great contentment and safety, as in the Nine of Earth. Nines can feel like a completion, but really they're the moment just before we've finished our journey. Many Nines in a reading indicate someone who feels a desire to move forward—but not quite yet.

TEN CARDS

Tens are true endings that lead to new beginnings. Often they bring about a sense of completion with the issues of a particular suit before moving on to another suit. However, sometimes they lead right back to the Ace of the same suit if the client doesn't feel finished with those issues. Tens can bring with them a sense of contentment and happiness, as in the Ten of Water or the Ten of Earth. The Ten of Air and the Ten of Fire may bring "contentment," but it's more often in the form of relief that a situation has finally come to an end. Either way, the opportunities for new beginnings are immense. Multiple Tens are signs that a client is ready to move on.

~

Keep in mind that each of the pip cards follows the energy of its suit. For example, Aces are about beginnings, so the Ace of Air might represent a new idea or the beginning of an intellectual pursuit. The Ace of Water, however, is more likely to signify the start of a new relationship or something we feel very emotional about. Fours relate to stability and structure. The Four of Fire indicates joy and celebration with respect to our accomplishments, while the Four of Earth shows pride in our financial security.

Another interesting thing to note is when we see the same series of numbers in multiple readings. If we were to receive, for example, the Two of Fire followed by the Four of Water and then the Seven of Earth, that's a series of 2-4-7. If, in a later reading, we get that same series of numbers but with different cards, then it may be time to look up 247 in numerology as a part of that reading.

The Court Cards

The Minor Arcana court cards include a Page, a Knight, a Queen, and a King. There is one of each of those cards in every Minor Arcana suit, and they can represent either a situation or a person during a reading. In the *Angel Tarot Cards,* information regarding both people and situations are listed on the face of each court card.

At the top of the court cards are the personality traits attributed to that card when it refers to a person. This can be someone we know, a new person coming into our lives, or even ourselves. Sometimes we may realize that the card relates to a particular individual not because of the words at the top of the card, but because the character in the image actually *looks* like someone we know. This is perfectly acceptable, and something that everyone should trust their intuition about.

Historically in tarot, Pages and Queens have been female, and Knights and Kings have been male. In the *Angel Tarot Cards,* this tradition is followed, but that's not something anyone must feel tied to. For example, if the personality traits of the King of Earth sound very much like a woman we know, then we can feel comfortable in allowing that card to represent her. There are only 16 court cards, and it would be redundant to have a male and a female image representing all the possible sets of personalities. Allow your intuition to choose without worrying too much about the gender of the person portrayed on the card.

At the bottom of the court cards are key phrases, much the same as those found on the pip cards and the Major Arcana. These reflect situations or actions that our angels are communicating with us about.

Perhaps one of the most commonly asked questions about tarot is: "How do I know whether a court card in the reading is reflecting a person or a situation?"

First, look for context. The words "their" and "they're" sound exactly the same in a sentence, but we know which word the speaker intended by the context in which the word was used. The same is true for court cards. Readings usually tell a story, so if a court card shows up in a spread that was giving the client advice on what to do next, it may seem out of context for that card to suddenly drop in on another person. But the advice on the bottom of the card may flow perfectly with the rest of that reading.

On the other hand, if clients have asked questions about their hope for impending romance, it may make perfect sense in the reading for tarot to be describing a person they're going to meet— or even someone they know who has a friend they could introduce them to!

You should also keep in mind that the court cards are very much like the suits they represent.

— The **Fire** court cards tend to be dramatic, optimistic, fiery, and full of action. They have a plan, and their hearts are really in it! Working with them often yields incredible accomplishments (and they make it fun, as well). Likewise, their relationships tend to be wildly passionate and exciting.

— The court cards of the **Water** suit are deeply emotional. They are the nurturers of the tarot and see to everyone's needs with great care and kindness. (Well, except their own. They often completely forget to take care of themselves.) When they fall in love, they really *fall* in love! They're also very intuitive.

— The **Air** court cards are more cerebral, intellectual, and stoic. They understand the world through the wisdom of experience, and therefore are extremely capable and often quite witty. They can also be emotionally unavailable.

— Finally, the **Earth** court cards are "salt of the earth" types. Practical, stable, and dependable, they're people you can rely on. Even the Page is mature beyond her years, and unlike the other Knights, the Knight of Earth will make a plan before just flying into action. They're generally very successful in life and can be quite ambitious (usually in a good way). They're very focused on their families as well as their activism.

There are also common traits among each court-card type:

Page Cards

Pages often reflect a new beginning. Generally they love to learn and are anxious to apply what they've discovered so far out in the "real world." Due to their lack of experience, they can be both excited and uncertain about how things will turn out. Depending on their suit, they may be raring to go (Page of Fire) or shy and nervous (Page of Water). They may display endless curiosity (Page of Earth) or be very detail oriented (Page of Air). Regardless of their suit, they bring a youthfulness to the table that may be indicative of the age of the person reflected, or how new a project is that's being referenced.

Pages also often represent messengers or messages that relate to their suit. The Page of Air might represent someone who has an important intellectual message for us, but who also communicates in a harsh manner. Although the Page of Earth could represent a legal contract or an acceptance into a university, the Page of Water can indicate a love letter or an invitation to a social event—while the Page of Fire may show up in the form of a job offer.

KNIGHT CARDS

Knights are focused on action and getting things done. They love a quest and want to help. Sometimes their energy is swift and decisive (and perhaps even a bit impulsive), like the Knight of Air. Or the pace could be a lot slower, like the Knight of Earth (although sometimes slow and steady can win the race!). The Knight of Water acts upon affairs in an emotional way, while the Knight of Fire is all about passion. Again, how each Knight goes about a task depends on the energy of the suit. What we can be assured of is that Knights will accomplish great things.

While all the Knights care that a particular job gets done, the energy of the suit can also shed light on their motives for caring. The Knight of Fire gets excited by the challenge and wants to test his skills. The Knight of Air sees the accomplishment as an intellectual exercise. The Knight of Earth wants to build something important for a friend or humankind, and the Knight of Water takes up the quest because of love or other emotions.

QUEEN CARDS

Queens are the nurturers of the tarot. Loving and supportive, they not only want to help us, but are also extremely capable of doing so. They're generally multitalented, multifaceted individuals who feel deeply about those around them, their situation, and any challenges they may be encountering.

Just like the other court cards, each of the Queens has motivations and skill sets that correlate to her suit. The Queen of Fire is able to accomplish just about anything. Her ability to multitask is astonishing, which allows her to be a great mother, a wonderful spouse, and an amazing employee all rolled up into one. The Queen of Water is a deeply loving and intuitive person who will give until she has nothing left. Her spiritual insights are often amazing "Aha!" moments. The Queen of Air has seen it all—she's experienced just about everything in life. Her sense of humor is sharp and keen, and she can provide great counsel. She's also often single, having tried her hand at love and found it not to be to her tastes. And then there's the Queen of Earth. She's very concerned about hearth and home and is usually an amazing housekeeper. She also has admirable financial skills.

KING CARDS

Kings are authority figures. They're generally our employers, supervisors, or the parent at home who wields the power. They're masters at making decisions, delegating tasks, and successfully administrating just about anything from building a bridge to organizing a shoe closet. If a King shows up with advice in a reading, we really should take it!

Kings represent the energy of their suit. The King of Fire is often center stage in one way or another. He may be the president of a dynamic company or the star of a play. The King of Water is a man you can trust in a relationship. He has depth of emotion that's been tested by time, which has allowed him to develop an undeniable integrity. The King of Air is brilliant! His ideas are always perfect for the situation, and his ability to communicate them is unsurpassed. Finally, the King of Earth is an amazing father who provides financial security for his family, and usually has the ability to turn any project into a prosperous venture.

CHAPTER SIX

SYMBOLISM
and NAMING

Tarot is a divination tool that's rich with symbolism. The *Angel Tarot Cards* continue this tradition, and only include positive and life-affirming symbols. As discussed earlier, a large portion of the imagery you see in traditional tarot cards has been handed down from one deck to another for centuries—oftentimes with very little change.

While there's a substantial amount of traditional symbolism in the *Angel Tarot Cards,* there's also a significant amount of new imagery as well. The reason these changes were made was to create a deck that was gentler and more accessible to everyone, without diluting the message of any individual card.

Likewise, some of the names of the cards in the Major Arcana have been changed for the same reason. Traditional tarot cards featured words that were very jarring to look at and that were somewhat frightening. More often than not, the troubling name had little to do with the actual meaning of the card in modern times. The names of some cards were changed as well, purely for clarity. There's nothing particularly wrong with the card name Temperance, for example, but the word itself is archaic and unfamiliar to modern people. So why use it when Balance conveys the meaning of the card without the need to look it up in a dictionary?

A good example of the type of changes made in the imagery and naming can be found in the first card of the *Angel Tarot Cards*. In traditional tarot, Card 0 is named The Fool and portrays a youth who's unfocused to the point that there's a risk of falling off a cliff. Nipping at The Fool's heels is a dog who doesn't seem to be working in concert with the youth. The very name of the card tends to indicate someone who's about to do something extremely unwise while getting himself injured at the same time.

The card called The Dreamer was chosen as a replacement for The Fool in the *Angel Tarot Cards* for a variety of reasons. First, the Major Arcana represents our incarnation into this life, and as such, presents us with endless possibilities for creation. Naming the card The Dreamer was meant to represent someone with the ability to dream big dreams and make the most of every opportunity. It reflects someone who can take that leap of faith and bring about true change in the world. Many people also see life on Earth as being something of a dream that our souls are experiencing, which further gave credence to that new name.

The new vision for this card maintains its original meaning, without the demeaning term of "fool" leading to a misunderstanding. After all, the 0 card traditionally means hope, faith, and opportunity. These aren't foolish qualities at all!

As for the imagery, it seeemed unnecessary to show the youth as being in danger. So the card was reimagined to show The Dreamer passing through an energy portal while standing on solid ground. The dog nipping at the heels of the traditional fool is now the young person's equal partner in the adventure. Additional imagery of a crane, a Pegasus, butterflies, and a unicorn were also added, giving our Dreamer card depth of meaning, as well as the significant symbolism that the traditional Fool card presented. (For more on The Dreamer card's meaning, see page 70.)

When symbolism was removed from any particular card, imagery of equivalent significance was put back into the card in its place. The depth and variety of human experience wasn't removed when the *Angel Tarot Cards* were created. Instead, the messages were simply made accessible so you could work with them without fear or worry. I couldn't see any benefits in tarot cards providing people with an accurate divination tool that elicited too much fear for the message to be understood!

CHAPTER SEVEN

ARCHANGELS, ANGEL NUMBERS, *and* ASTROLOGY

In Part III and Part IV of this book, you are provided with a lot of information on each card. In addition to The Dreamer's Journey and the in-depth symbolism presented in each image, you'll find material on the astrological attributions and angel numbers for each card, and insight about the archangels that you'll find in the Major Arcana.

Here are a few summaries to help make each section clear as you read Parts III and IV.

The Archangels

Archangels are messengers of the Divine who give us guidance and assistance when we ask for it. It's particularly important to tell our archangels and angels that we want their help, as they won't intervene in our lives without being asked (except in the case of life-threatening situations). There are 15 primary archangels with different specialties, who each resonate with a particular aura or halo color.

For the Major Arcana of the *Angel Tarot Cards,* an archangel appears in every image based on his or her expertise and how each relates to the message of the card.

Angel Numbers

Angel numbers are a wonderful way for people who are more analytical than intuitive, or just starting to develop their intuition, to get messages from their angels. These are numbers that show up in sequences that people experience over and over. For example, you may wake up and notice that it's 5:47 A.M. Later in the day, you stop at the store and your purchases total $5.47. In front of you on the way home is a car with a license plate with the numbers 547 on it. Then you walk in your front door and see that you've arrived home at exactly 5:47 P.M.!

This is a very common phenomenon, and each of those number sequences has a specific meaning. The particular sequence 547 means "Congratulations for talking to your angels, listening to their guidance, and getting yourself on the right path."

In this part of the book, you will learn the angel number of each card in the *Angel Tarot Cards* and the meaning behind that number. Numbers were assigned to the Major Arcana based on the number of that card. The Minor Arcana were numbered in order based on the traditional order of Fire, Water, Air, and Earth cards.

You'll also find information on the numbers that each card reduces down to. Reduction is a traditional numerology concept that states that there is meaning in the number, as well as meaning in what the numbers add up to.

For example, the number 547 reduces down to 7 (5 + 4 + 7 = 16, 1 + 6 = 7). The numbers 11, 22, and 33 are considered master numbers and are not reduced beyond that point.

Astrology

Astrology is an ancient metaphysical science in which meaning is attributed to the placement of the Sun, Moon, and planets in the sky at the time of a significant moment in life. The sky is divided into 12 sections—each one reflecting a sign of the zodiac. In the late 19th century, astrological associations to cards of the tarot were made by certain spiritual groups.

Within the Major Arcana, a single planet or zodiac sign is assigned to each card. For example, The Empress is associated with Venus, while Balance is connected to Sagittarius.

Aces and Pages aren't connected to a specific planet or sign, but instead represent the pure energy of their element—such as Fire, Water, Air, or Earth.

Pip cards Two through Ten have very specific attributions that include a planet and a zodiac sign. The Six of Fire reflects Jupiter in Leo, while the Three of Water is Mercury in Cancer.

Most people have had the experience of engaging in a conversation that goes something like this: "Hi, I'm a Taurus! What's *your* sign?" This is referring to the person's "Sun sign"; however, astrology is a very complex science that represents the intricacies of human beings. In that same vein, the court cards Knight, Queen, and King are reflected by two signs—though one more so than the other. For example, the Queen of Fire is Aries with a bit of Pisces thrown in, while the King of Earth is Virgo with a splash of Leo.

CHAPTER EIGHT

HOW *to* GIVE *a* READING

Everyone is born with intuitive gifts from Source. How in tune people are with those gifts is determined by many factors, such as experiences from their childhood, how those gifts are viewed by others, their romantic partners' opinions, and other societal influences. For example, if a boy's parents are especially supportive of him taking action based on his intuition, then that boy is likely to grow up very connected to his inner guidance.

The wonderful thing to remember is that our gifts never go away. We may not hear the whispers of our angels, but all of us can wake up and reconnect with our intuitive nature. Therefore, anyone can have an angel tarot card reading and get insightful, accurate, and healing information for themselves or others.

To help you get started, I've outlined a few steps on how to give a successful reading.

Energetically Clear Your Card Deck

Your cards are very sensitive instruments—that's what makes them work so well! So it's very common for them to pick up energy from other people during the process of manufacturing and shipping.

To clear your cards, first hold the deck in your nondominant hand (the hand you normally don't write with), as this is the hand that *receives* energy. Hold your other hand (the one that sends energy) over the deck and imagine white light leaving your palm and going into the deck. Then think the thought that you'd like the cards to be cleared, and say a prayer over the cards, such as:

*"Dear Universe, thank you for lifting away
anything from these cards that is not of Divine love."*

This clears the cards and prepares them to receive your unique energy.

Consecrate the Cards

Briefly touch each of the cards to infuse them with your personal energy. Think of this as saying "Hello" to each card. You can simply touch a corner of each one to accomplish this. Then fan the cards out with the artwork facing you. Hold the fanned cards to your heart and think about any prayers or intentions you'd like to bestow upon them. For instance, you can say the following, silently or aloud:

"I ask that all of my readings with these cards be accurate and specific, and bring blessings to everyone involved. Please help me stay centered in my higher self so that I may clearly hear, see, feel, and know the Divine messages that wish to come through these readings."

Ask and pray for whatever help you'd like during your readings—such as confidence, clarity, compassion, and so forth. Your cards now carry your personal vibration and intentions.

You'll need to clear and consecrate your cards anytime you allow someone else to touch them. There may also be times when your readings begin to lack clarity after you've done a lot of them. This just means that the cards need to be cleared and consecrated again.

Ask a Question

Think of a question you'd like an answer to. If you're giving a reading for someone, ask him or her to either think of or verbalize a question. Your angels and guides can hear your thoughts, so you needn't voice your queries aloud.

Shuffle the Cards

Think of the question as you shuffle the cards, and ask the angels to help you with answers and guidance. I often say this prayer while shuffling the cards:

"Dear angels, I ask that you be sure that only your pure and trustworthy messages come through these cards. Please protect my loved ones and me. Please help me to see, hear, feel, and know the messages that you have for us. I ask that this card reading bring blessings to everyone involved."

If one or more cards "jump" out of the deck while you're shuffling, place them to the side. They'll be part of your reading.

As you're shuffling, you'll probably notice feelings, thoughts, words, or visions. This Divine guidance will help you further understand the cards you draw, so pay attention to these impressions as they come to you.

When your cards begin to clump into two distinct sections, it's time to stop shuffling. You may also receive a feeling, thought, or vision to cease—or you may even hear the words *Stop shuffling now.* Trust and honor these Divine messages that are helping you with the reading. You can't make a mistake and stop shuffling too soon or late, as the Law of Attraction ensures that you'll always choose the correct cards.

Lay Out the Cards

Draw as many cards from the deck as are needed for the spread you're using. Some people pull their cards from the top of the deck, and others randomly choose from the stack. You can't select the wrong card, so don't worry about that! The cards that you pick are the answer to your question, or guidance about which healing steps to take to help you with the issue you've inquired about.

Review the Information Regarding the Cards

Turn to the corresponding page for each card in Part III or IV of this book. The information there will give you specific guidance to help walk you through any life changes, or take appropriate action. As you read the words, notice any thoughts or feelings that come to you, as they're a personalized part of the answer.

Listen to Your Intuition

As you read the words on the cards, continue to notice any thoughts, additional words, feelings, or visions that come to you, as these are messages from your angels and guides that personalize the card's particular meaning for you. The images on the *Angel Tarot Cards* are rich with detail and symbolism, so they're just as much a part of the reading as the words. If you set aside a card (or cards) that "jumped" out of the deck while you were shuffling, carefully examine it, too.

All information that the angels bring forth should be shared during the reading even if your ego tries to convince you that it can't possibly be correct. You may very well be denying your clients important guidance if you allow a lack of confidence to keep you from sharing everything you get in a reading. Even if clients don't see the relevance of the information right away, often it will become apparent to them shortly thereafter.

Believe in Yourself!

As you practice giving yourself and others readings, you'll become more and more confident. Your connection to your intuitive gifts will grow stronger, and you'll realize just how powerful your inner guidance is. Be gentle with yourself as you grow in your skills, and trust the information the angels impart to you.

PART II

The MAGIC *of* SPREADS

CHAPTER NINE

CREATING YOUR OWN SPREADS

One of the most important parts of any angel tarot card reading is the spread, a pattern of laying out cards where specific positions provide insight into various aspects of the question being asked. Certainly, one of the most famous spreads of all is the Celtic Cross. This ten-card spread offers great detail on any topic, including the basis of the situation; aspects that are "crossing" or affecting it; and the recent past, present, future, and so on.

What many people may not know is that creating your own spread is rewarding, fun, and quite easy. Much like all aspects of giving or receiving a reading, it just takes a bit of intuition and practice. There are five basic things to consider when creating a spread. They are:

- Grounding and asking for guidance

- Understanding the purpose of the spread

- Determining the number of cards in the layout

- Creating the shape or layout of the spread

- Deciding what each card's position represents

Grounding and Guidance

Every aspect of doing intuitive work is aided by taking a moment to become grounded and to engage in a meditation with the specific archangels who can help you with your task. This is certainly true when creating a new spread. As an example, consider inviting four archangels to ground the space in the four corners of the room you're working in.

Anyone can follow their intuition as to which four archangels to invite, but here are some examples:

- Archangel Gabriel, to help with creative projects

- Archangel Uriel, to provide enlightenment and epiphanies

- Archangel Haniel, to help with intuitive abilities

- Archangel Michael, to provide a sense of Divine safety and security during any task

It doesn't matter which archangels you choose or which corner they stand in. All that matters is that you allow your intuition to guide you.

The Purpose

Once you've said a prayer for insight and guidance, it's time to consider what the purpose of the spread is going to be. Is it about romance? Are you seeking insight into a career concern? Is the spread even for a particular topic, or is it more of a general spread that can be used in any situation?

For example, included in Chapter 10 is a spread called "Plan B." The purpose of this spread is for those times when things just aren't going the way you were hoping they would and you need guidance on what to do next. This spread can be used for any topic, and is meant to get your dreams moving again!

The "Loving Heart" spread (also in Chapter 10) is mainly intended to give you insight into romantic or other intimate relationships. However, in truth, with just a little tweaking, you could use it for any situation where two people (a sibling, a boss or supervisor, and so on) are involved.

The Number of Cards

The next step is to decide how many cards will be in the spread. One way is to ask your angels and accept the first number that pops into your mind as Divine guidance. For example, if the number 7 suddenly enters your awareness, then you might start with a seven-card spread.

Another way to choose the number of cards in a spread is to jot down on a piece of paper all the questions that someone might have on the topic. For example, if the spread is designed for relationship issues, some common questions might include:

- How does the other person feel about me?

- Is this relationship in my highest and greatest good?

- Does this relationship have a promising future, or is it temporary?

Try to come up with questions that will provide the type of detailed insight someone longing for answers about a relationship would want. The number of questions may determine the number of cards. Spreads that are ten cards or fewer can offer a great deal of detail without becoming cumbersome. (Sometimes less really is more.) Still, no matter if it's 2, 8, or 20 cards, just follow your intuition!

Finally, another way to come up with the number of cards for a spread is to use the *Angel Tarot Cards, Archangel Power Tarot Cards, Guardian Angel Tarot Cards,* or any deck that has numbers on the face. For example, pulling "7 – The Chariot" would indicate a seven-card spread since that's the number at the top of the card. Drawing a higher card like "19 – The Sun" might indicate that the number should be reduced, as discussed in Chapter 7. A spread with 19 cards would be a very large spread, indeed! If that feels like more cards than is appropriate, then reduce the numbers by adding the 1 + 9, and see if ten cards feels more manageable.

No matter how you come up with the number, be open to change. Sometimes we can get to the end of creating a particular spread only to realize that there are more (or fewer) positions than first anticipated. Allow the power of creativity and intuition to adjust the number up or down as necessary.

The Shape

Once the purpose of the spread and the number of cards have been determined, it's time to decide what shape it's going to take. Spreads are made up of anything from straight rows of cards, shapes such as squares or circles, or even symbols that represent the purpose. A romance spread might be shaped like a heart, or if the topic of the spread is career, then it might make sense to lay it out in a star shape and call it "The Rising Star."

Think about having certain cards cross one another, much like cards 1 and 2 of the Celtic Cross (see page 58). Generally the card that's lying horizontally across the vertical card is said to be affecting whatever the vertical card represents. However, it can represent whatever the angels tell you it means. Creating a spread is all about intention. We tell Heaven or the angels how we want the message to come to us, and they gladly follow along!

The Meanings

Finally, it will be necessary to decide what each position of the spread pertains to. If the questions for the spread have been created as a way to determine the number of cards to use, then a lot of the work will have already been done. If not, now is the time to make those decisions. Write down a list of questions, and then try to place them in a logical order, where each one relates to the question before it.

As an example, a career spread might read as follows:

- How does my client feel about her career right now?

- Is it time for a change in career for her?

- What type of work would make her most happy?

- How might she go about getting the perfect job?

- Would my client do well being self-employed?

- What is the final outcome of this situation?

It's fairly common for the last card of a spread to be a "Final Outcome" card. This just gives recipients of a reading an idea of where their current situations are headed.

Remember that as in all readings, there's always free will. Sometimes the angel tarot cards are giving us a heads-up that the direction in which we're going might not make us happy, thereby allowing us to change it.

The next step is to take each question and assign it to one of the positions that was created for the shape of the spread. Feel free to experiment with this. If the first attempt to attribute a card to a particular position seems awkward when you try out the spread, then be open to moving the questions around until the reading feels smooth and easy.

Practice, Practice, Practice!

Now it's time to take the new spread for a test drive! It's a good idea to try the spread on several people to see how it goes. Feel free to make changes to the spread as it becomes clear what does and doesn't work. Add or subtract a card if it isn't working in its original format, or even change the shape or the specific questions in the spread.

Another great way to test a spread is to post it online at Facebook.com/CertifiedAngelCardReaders. There are thousands of people in that community just waiting to provide feedback on how a spread is working. Everyone loves to see a new spread on that page, so do share it with us!

CHAPTER TEN

SAMPLE SPREADS

Here are a few sample spreads. Some of these are ideal for quick and easy answers, and others are useful for more in-depth insights. In order to avoid confusion, for the most part the word *client* will be used to reflect the person getting the reading even if that person is *you*.

One-Card Readings

One-card readings are useful as a tool for learning how to use angel tarot cards. Consider choosing one card at the beginning of every day, and then compare that card's message to the events that you experience.

Sometimes when I am in a hurry, I'll just ask a quick question and pull a single card to receive instant advice.

Simple Yes/No Answers

There are an endless number of complicated spreads in books and on the Internet showing how to get a simple yes-or-no answer to a question from tarot. In truth, there's a very simple way to get a response.

Think of the question you want an answer to while shuffling. When you feel compelled to stop, take the top card from the deck. Most cards in tarot have a *positive* energy or a *challenging* energy. Positive cards would reflect a *yes,* while challenging cards indicate a *no.*

For example, the Nine of Water is a very positive card that indicates wishes coming true, so it makes sense to see this card as a *yes.* The Five of Air is a card that indicates an unwise choice, so it's easy to see that card as a *no.*

While yes-or-no questions can be very tempting to ask, keep in mind that tarot is always trying to help us out. There are many positive cards and challenging cards, so I encourage everyone to look at the card and then consider why tarot offered that *particular* card as the answer. For example, the Nine of Water and The Chariot are both very positive cards, but the former indicates getting what we want very easily, while the latter implies success that comes through hard work.

Timing Questions

Another frequent question that clients ask is "when" a particular event will occur. One of the advantages of tarot cards in answering such questions is that they're numbered.

To get an idea of when something is going to happen, ask the question in your mind while shuffling. When you get the message to stop, take the top card from the deck. Let's say that the card is the Three of Earth. The basis of the timing is the number 3. This is where intuition comes into play. Hold the card and ask your angels, "Is it three days?" An immediate feeling or knowing will come that says *yes* or *no.* Then ask, "Is it three weeks?" and again, an answer will come. Follow that with months or years. Don't forget that the answer could also signify the third of a particular month.

Another method is to look at the card for indicators of the time of year. For example, the Ace of Earth presents an autumn scene, while the Page of Air has a distinct feeling of winter to it.

(If you're interested in a simple oracle focused on straight-forward answers, especially to yes-or-no and timing questions, check out my *Angel Answers Oracle Cards*.)

Three-Card Spread

A very common spread that people turn to is one involving three cards. The cards are laid out left to right, and are then read in that same order.

Card 1 gives us information about how the past may be influencing the question at hand.

Card 2 speaks to us about the present situation and how the client is experiencing these circumstances.

Card 3 tells us about the most likely outcome of the situation if no action to change things is taken.

Celtic Cross

Without question, the Celtic Cross is one of the most well-known and treasured card spreads in tarot, as it can be used to answer questions about any topic. This spread of ten cards reveals the basis of your situation, the challenges, the past, the present, the near future, and the likely outcome.

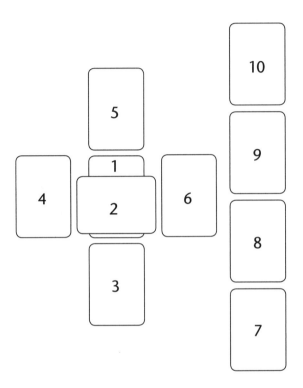

Card 1 represents the present moment. It can refer to those getting a reading or the primary concerns on their minds.

Card 2 represents the current challenge affecting Card 1. It can indicate a block that keeps a situation from getting resolved or moving forward, or it may signify the cause of the challenge that the client is experiencing at the moment.

Card 3 represents the basis or "foundation" of the question. This may be linked to subconscious influences imposed by someone involved (including the client), information that this person is keeping quiet due to embarrassment, or experiences from the distant past that are still affecting the client in the present day.

Card 4 represents the recent past relevant to the situation. This can also indicate a situation that has come to a conclusion in a way that the client may judge to be good or not so good.

Card 5 represents the present. This card may also signify what clients feel they're able to accomplish or are hoping to achieve. If Card 3 is the subconscious, then Card 5 is the conscious.

Card 6 represents the near future. It's often an event or a shift in the energy of the situation. It can also indicate someone new who's going to come into the person's life bearing on the question being asked.

Card 7 represents one's power in a situation. If the card that's showing is a strong, empowering card, then clients are maintaining their personal power. If the card is one that is challenging or difficult, then it may be that the clients have relinquished control to someone else. This can also shed light on how clients see themselves at the moment.

Card 8 represents the effects of other people. It often refers to friends, family, people at work, or anyone who's involved with the question. It can also be an indicator of how other individuals see the client.

Card 9 represents hopes or fears. This position indicates whether clients have a strong belief that things will work out, or are living in fear that they won't. In much the same way as Card 7, positive cards indicate someone who has great hope. Challenging cards may indicate negative thoughts that are impacting the situation.

Card 10 represents the outcome. If no action is taken to change the situation, then this card indicates what to expect as the likely result. However, we must always remember that we have free will. If we don't like the direction in which things are headed, then we can and must change our path!

Loving Heart Spread

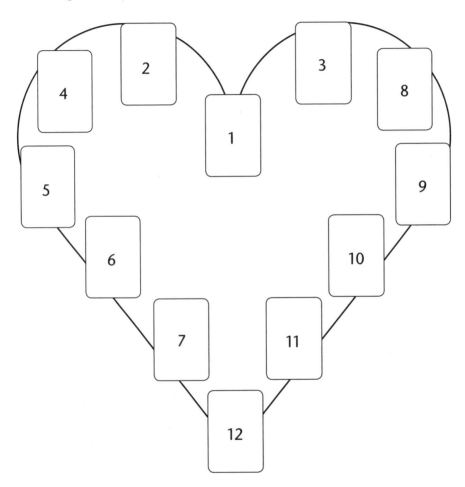

This is a wonderful spread for relationships of any kind. While it does lend itself to romantic relationships, it can just as easily be used for getting clarity on a client's situation with a parent, sibling, friend, or boss.

The first matter of business is to establish who in the relationship is person A, and who is person B. It's very important to have that firmly in mind before beginning. If the purpose of this reading is to look at any future relationships of a single person, then person A should be the client, and person B should be the incoming partner.

Card 1 provides an immediate overview of what's going on between the parties. A positive card tells us that the relationship is doing well, while a challenging card would tell us where things are going wrong. It may also tell us *why*.

Card 2 tells us the ways in which the relationship is strong.

Card 3 gives us insight into how the relationship is currently being challenged.

Card 4 is person A's hopes for the relationship.

Card 5 enlightens us to person A's true feelings regarding person B.

Card 6 shows us the way in which person A is adversely affecting the relationship.

Card 7 gives suggestions as to how person A could be of help to person B.

Card 8 indicates person B's hopes for the relationship.

Card 9 reveals person B's true feelings for person A.

Card 10 tells us how person B is adversely affecting the relationship.

Card 11 offers insight into how person B could help person A.

Card 12 tells us the most likely scenario regarding the future of the relationship if no changes are made.

Once you've read the cards all the way around the heart, it can be fascinating to then go back and look vertically across the heart. Compare Card 4 (person A's hopes for the relationship) to Card 8 (person B's hopes). Likewise, you can compare Cards 5 and 9, 6 and 10, and 7 and 11. This provides excellent insight into how each person is operating in the relationship and where there are imbalances.

Career: X Marks the Spot!

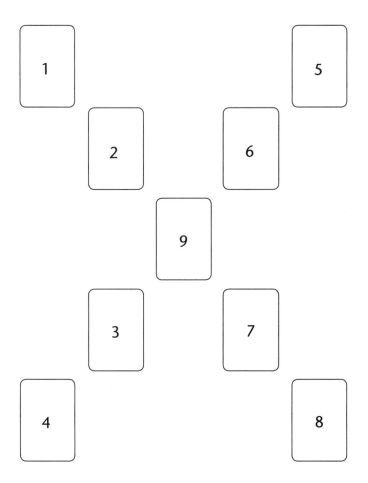

Career is definitely one of the most asked-about topics in a reading. It can be challenging for clients to determine if they should make changes to better their current situation, move on to a different job, or even try a totally new career.

Since finding the answer can be like searching for buried treasure, this spread is called "X Marks the Spot," and it's meant to help clients in their search for meaning and joy in their jobs. The cards are laid out in the form of an "X." The left side of the spread leans toward the energy of the current job or career; making a change is represented on the right side.

Card 1 gives us insight into how happy or unhappy clients are in their current position. Is there joy in what they do? Or have things become humdrum or even miserable?

Card 2 tells us how clients' current careers or jobs differ from what they'd hoped for. Had they anticipated something more exciting? More creative?

Card 3 offers advice on how clients might improve their current work situations. Perhaps there are people where they work who could help them move up the ladder. Or would getting more training or education be helpful?

Card 4 speaks of the advantages to clients remaining in their current positions. This card could indicate that there's a new and exciting opportunity about to open up where they currently work. Or they might be about to make an important new connection that could lead to a better job later on.

Card 5 lets us know if this is a good time for clients to pursue a different job or to make a career transition. It can also indicate that this is a poor time to make a change.

Card 6 reveals whether clients' ideas for making the change reflected by Card 5 would be in their best interests. Will the career they have in mind make them happy? Do they have a balanced and logical plan?

Card 7 tells us if clients would do well by becoming self-employed. Perhaps they'd benefit more by working with an established company.

Card 8 gives us insight into what type of work clients would most enjoy. Look for indicators of creative endeavors, healing practices, or more scientific professions that might bring them the most happiness.

Card 9 tells us the single most important action clients should take at this moment regarding their careers. It may indicate going back to school, updating their résumés, or even having a heart-to-heart chat with a current supervisor.

Healthy Steps Spread

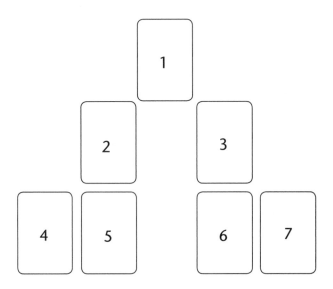

Another popular topic for people getting readings relates to health. This spread is called the "Healthy Steps" spread because its shape brought to mind the traditional food pyramid. So when the cards were laid out, they just naturally created a set of stairs on either side that can be seen as the steps to healthier clients.

Card 1 in this spread reflects the current condition of the person inquiring about health concerns. There are certain cards in tarot that speak to a particular health issue. For example, the Three of Air often indicates a heart condition, and the Ten of Fire may suggest chronic back pain. However, it's not uncommon to draw a card that doesn't signify anything specific. As we progress through the reading, clients' concerns will reveal themselves. If there's a person in the imagery on the card you've chosen for your client, note where on the body your eyes are drawn. Trust your intuition!

Card 2 shows the physical elements that are impacting a person's health. Examples of these include the Eight of Air, indicating great stress, while the Nine of Air shows sleep deprivation. The Chariot might indicate that physical ailments were caused by an automobile accident, while the Ego card may indicate substance-abuse problems.

Card 3 gives us insight into any emotional concerns that are impacting a client's health. For example, the Queen of Water would tell you that your client is giving entirely too much to others without leaving any time or energy for him- or herself. The Six of Water immediately suggests childhood issues or unresolved baggage from the past.

Card 4 reflects who could be of assistance in the client's search for better health. Court cards tend to fall into this position, but not always. Physical characteristics of a person who can help are sometimes garnered from a Major Arcana or pip card in the same way they can be from a court card.

Cards 5 tells us what the next step is to better health. The Five of Fire indicates that someone needs to get some exercise, while the Four of Air would suggest that a vacation may be long overdue. The King of Air indicates the need to consult a specialist.

Card 6 indicates the prospects for improvement over the short term.

Card 7 provides a more long-term prognosis.

Plan B Spread

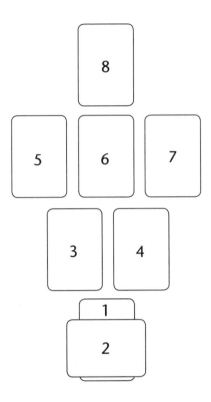

For those situations when it just doesn't seem like things are going the way we were hoping they would, here's a spread to lend insight into changes that could help get things going again.

Card 1 in this spread reflects what it is you're trying to accomplish. Think of it as validation that tarot understands the question.

Card 2 is laid out to cross Card 1. It represents the experience you're having in your attempts to accomplish your goal. Even a card that often has a positive feel can give you insight into what's getting in your way. For example, the Three of Water card often means celebration, but in position 2 of this spread, it might indicate that your friends are distracting you from getting your work done.

Card 3 talks about what I like to call "earthly challenges." Situations that fall into that category include not having enough money or feeling a lack of support from loved ones or business partners.

Card 4 represents unconscious hurdles. Consider: Are you self-sabotaging? Do you lack the passion and drive to succeed in this endeavor? If you're completely honest with yourself, is this even the goal you're setting for yourself?

Cards 5, 6, and 7 offer information on changes that would benefit your plan. You might find cards in this series that provide advice, such as not trying to do everything yourself, networking with others, or meditating daily in order to get the insights you lack.

Card 8 shows you the kinds of results you can expect by implementing your "Plan B."

PART III

The DREAMER'S JOURNEY THROUGH the MAJOR ARCANA

The Dreamer

The Dreamer is the first card of the Major Arcana, and the beginning of what I call The Dreamer's Journey. When this card appears, we're encouraged to take a leap of faith. Unexpected opportunities may present themselves, and there are endless possibilities for creating something wonderful. We may find a new project that we have a great passion for, or our own development and growth may be our "project." Problems will most easily be resolved via creative solutions. This is a card of promise and hope!

The Dreamer's Journey

This is where our magical journey begins. A choice is made to create something new or to pursue an entirely new phase of life. The story of The Dreamer begins when we choose our path with great optimism and hope. You see, we must realize that on this journey, whoever is getting the reading *is* The Dreamer! We may not be entirely sure why we're here on Earth or what we're going to accomplish, but we'll receive clarity as we go forward on our quest, visiting all the magical people of the Major Arcana along our way. So get ready to meet some amazing individuals!

This card also has a streak of independence around it and can indicate those who are leaving jobs they no longer enjoy or teenagers departing home to go off on their own.

Symbolism

While The Dreamer card draws its symbolism from the metaphor of the incarnation of a soul, it usually represents the beginning of *any* situation or phase in our lives.

A beautiful and confident young person is stepping through a portal into this world. The youth represented here reflects the newness of the situation, though not necessarily the age of the person who drew the card. The portal speaks of a doorway that leads from where our lives have taken us so far, to where we're currently building up the faith to go.

A dog accompanies The Dreamer on the journey to remind us that the world is full of animal souls, here to help us balance our experience and our understanding of our purpose. A dog was chosen because its emotional connection with, and loyalty to, humankind is legendary.

A butterfly zips through the portal with The Dreamer. Butterflies are a famous symbol of transformation due to their ability to evolve from caterpillars into beautiful winged creatures.

Cranes are symbols of reincarnation in many cultures, and there's evidence of them having been on Earth for more than 60 million years. Their wide wingspans are believed to be able to carry them to Heaven, and therefore to spiritual enlightenment. Pegasus is a winged horse who in mythology was said to be able to carry his rider from one plane to the next—just as our Dreamer is moving into a new phase of life.

Unicorns are beautiful, magical creatures of extreme purity of spirit whose energy can be a guide for how to be happy in our lives.

The city below The Dreamer is a construct of human development. It represents life on Earth as well as endless opportunities. The Dreamer is contemplating what might be created there.

Angel Number

In tarot, The Dreamer is number 0. This is a very mystical number that represents the Divine and eternity. It's a blank slate from which anything can be created—a cycle that begins, ends, and then begins again. It's perfect for a Dreamer who can reinvent him- or herself simply by having the faith to do so. Because The Dreamer card is considered both the beginning and the end of the Major Arcana, some also consider the card to be number 22.

Archangel

Archangel Metatron is known for watching over young people, as well as those who are seeking growth in their spirituality. When The Dreamer card represents a new project or endeavor, Metatron can also help with this "young" situation. Metatron presents himself in the colors violet and green.

Astrology

This card is associated with the planet Uranus, the symbol of which is on The Dreamer's jacket. It's a planet of creativity, independence, and innovation; it encourages us to be our own unique selves. It's associated with the energy of setting us free from old ideas or situations that no longer serve us.

~

1

The Magician
Archangel Raziel

You are ready! You have the resources or the ability to manifest them. Life is magical.

The Magician

When this card is drawn, we can be assured that we really do have what we need to move forward. We have the gifts and talents in this moment to be all that we want to be. The perception that we're lacking some key element or additional knowledge in order to be successful simply isn't true. What we need either is here right now or will magically appear soon.

The Magician doesn't guarantee that we're completely aware of what we *want* to accomplish, only that we could do just about anything we choose. Spiritually or subconsciously, we may be looking for someone impartial to help us understand our purpose. If we're already clear about our path, then this card demands "no more procrastination." Magical things will happen, but we must take the first steps!

The Dreamer's Journey

Next on the journey of The Dreamer, we encounter an incredible Magician! With his wise counsel, we come to realize that we have the ability to use the elements of this world to create the life we want. He teaches us that we're far more capable than we realize, and that we're born with the ability to accomplish great deeds. It doesn't matter whether we have everything planned out or not. The main point is that we believe in ourselves and our Divinely given right to make the most of whatever we choose to do with our lives.

Symbolism

The Magician wears the icons of the four elements on his belt: Fire, Air, Water, and Earth. These are the names of the suits in the Minor Arcana as well as the basic building blocks of the material aspects of living on Earth.

The Magician represents the concept of "as above, so below," and indeed, brings down the energy of Heaven to Earth. He has the ability to manifest his dreams through his positive thoughts.

Above The Magician's head floats the infinity sign, which is the number 8 lying on its side—another piece of evidence that our ability to manifest is eternal and unending.

In ancient tarot cards, The Magician is beneath an arbor of roses to symbolize that the information he has is secret. However, in the *Angel Tarot Cards,* I've chosen to reflect that the secrets behind this ancient mystical art are no longer hidden by showing

The Magician as having risen above the archway where the roses grow.

At his feet there's a field of lilies that represents the purity of his motivations. The Magician wants to create something wonderful and worthy of "Heaven on Earth."

Angel Number

In tarot, this card is number 1—a very powerful and creative number from which all beginnings spring forth. The energy of this number allows us to take action and achieve our independence, but we must be conscious of our thoughts in order to manifest the lives we want rather than those based on our fears.

Archangel

Archangel Raziel is an amazing wizard who sits at the throne of God and keeps a magical book of universal wisdom. Raziel's name means "the secrets of God," and he shows up in rainbow colors, as is represented by his halo and the magical energy he uses to fulfill his life purpose. He has the ability to take knowledge and transform it into reality. While his name implies secrets, he's very happy to share all he knows to help us have magical lives. He is the perfect magician for this card.

Astrology

This card is associated with the planet Mercury—which is all about communication and intellect. The Magician teaches us that anything we can think up, we can create! This is the basic Law of Attraction. By visualizing our dreams and then taking action, we can have the life we want to live. This is perfect for The Magician, who can get anything done!

∼

Listen to your intuition. Have patience.
Consider carefully what you want before acting.

The High Priestess

The High Priestess is a card of meditation and inner reflection. It invites us to be quiet by going within in order to get a clear understanding of ourselves and our desires. The clarity we gain assures us that once we do move into motion, we're headed in the right direction. Consider The High Priestess card as a permission slip to take some time to reflect upon what the angels have to say.

It's not necessary to take action with this card. In fact, it's best if we take our time. We're asked to follow our intuition and be patient with ourselves and others. The answers we seek will come at the perfect moment. Meanwhile, sometimes our answers come faster through keeping our ponderings to ourselves. This card may be telling our clients that some secrets are best left unshared.

The Dreamer's Journey

We can choose to take a leap of faith and know our own power, but without a clear understanding of what we want to create, we're just spinning our wheels. So next we meet The High Priestess. She is beautiful, wise, and a bit mysterious. She has explored her inner world in great detail and is highly skilled at understanding the spiritual voices of the angels. Under her guidance, we study meditation and learn to go within to find the answers to any questions that beckon us. We discover something about who we are, and the Divine life purpose we were born to live.

When The High Priestess feels that we're ready, she will send us on our way. We can't stay in meditation and contemplation forever if we are to create the lives we wish to live.

Symbolism

The High Priestess stands in front of two pillars, one lighter in color, the other much darker. They represent concepts such as positive and negative, male and female, conscious and subconscious. All options are possible between these extremes. What will we choose?

It's difficult to see what's behind The High Priestess, as her beautiful headdress blocks our view. This symbolizes that there are wonderful mysteries to be discovered through meditation and spiritual seeking.

The High Priestess wears a cross of equal proportions. It is perfectly balanced in height and length in order to convey the importance of not taking our beliefs to one extreme or another. Balance is a part of the path to peace.

Above her head shines the full Moon. All the emotional mysteries of what we might create are represented by the Moon. Its light shines as a reflection of the light that is within us.

The High Priestess holds open a book containing all the mystical knowledge of the Universe. Unlike in ancient tarot where this is a rolled-up scroll of hidden information, here The High Priestess is presented as freely offering up all of her secrets.

Her dress is turning to water before our eyes. Water is a traditional symbol of emotions, as well as the stream of consciousness that meditation and inner searching can provide us.

Angel Number

The High Priestess is Card 2. This number asks us to think positively. All will turn out well as long as we don't worry or show a lack of faith. And much like the two pillars behind The High Priestess, this number speaks of the duality of energies such as light and dark, male and female. It's also a number that seeks out peace and spirituality.

Archangel

Archangel Haniel is known for psychic gifts, intuition, and feminine energy. Her name means "the grace of God," and she is the perfect guide in our quest for inner knowledge. She's known for her association with the Moon, and is likewise tied to feminine issues. Her halo is pale blue.

Astrology

Astrologically, this card is related to the Moon, which is considered to be the ruler of our emotions as well as our personal needs. It gives us insight into how we feel about things and the types of people or topics we feel drawn to. Our personalities are determined by the Moon because it has such a powerful effect on our emotions, how we feel about ourselves, and our inner beliefs.

~

The Empress

When The Empress card is drawn, it's time to stop pondering our fate and get busy! It's a time of amazing prosperity, and we can be assured that we'll be very successful at everything we put our minds to. The Empress is a sure sign of the ability to manifest our dreams.

This card can be an indicator of impending pregnancy or the birth of a child (this can include adoption). Motherhood and maternal issues are also within The Empress's domain, so nurturing ourselves or those around us is something this card is very concerned with. However, we need to remember that "giving birth" can be a metaphor for beginning a beloved project or a new phase of our lives. Our "baby" might be a business we just opened or a book we're in the process of writing.

And while we're nurturing those around us, it's also just fine to do something luxurious for ourselves. We may spend time in nature, buy ourselves a beautiful piece of jewelry, or seek out healing experiences such as massage or Reiki.

The Dreamer's Journey

On the next step of the journey we meet The Empress. We've benefited from the quiet time we spent with The High Priestess, and now we're clear on what we want to do. The Empress teaches us to take action and to harness our self-confidence in order to create wonderful things. Many see her as the embodiment of Mother Nature, full of abundance and creativity. From her, we learn that we're able to do many things at once if we're committed and dedicated to our cause—which is incredibly exciting!

Her optimism is contagious, and suddenly we're raring to go—there's no more holding back. The Empress's ability to surround herself with luxurious and beautiful things also teaches us that by putting all our efforts and passion into our endeavors, we will be richly rewarded.

Symbolism

In the background of this card, we see a waterfall that pools into a stream leading toward The Empress. This is the water that came from the gown of The High Priestess, and it represents the physical manifestation of the epiphanies that we received during our time of meditation with her.

The Empress is surrounded by abundant life, including cypress trees that symbolize the strength of our convictions to achieve our goals.

In traditional tarot, The Empress is usually shown in a pregnant state to symbolize the amazing fertility and creativity of the moment; however, our empress is Archangel Gabriel, so here she is holding a baby instead. This shows that this is a moment of great opportunity for manifesting whatever we wish to create.

The butterflies are a symbol of evolution, since they can transform themselves from caterpillars into beautiful, winged creatures.

Surrounding The Empress are many symbols from nature. The baby bear reminds us of its magical ability to hibernate and then to reawaken in the spring. Our time of quiet with The High Priestess has past, and now we must wake up!

The tender nature of the deer reminds us to be kind to ourselves and others as we take on this new time of creation.

Squirrels are famous for gathering nuts to get ready for winter. They represent the need to be prepared, as well as an invitation to make our tasks playful and enjoyable.

The cougar is a very powerful animal that acts with confidence and self-assurance. It asks that we take charge of our own lives and not allow others to dissuade us from our goals.

Coyotes work in groups to accomplish goals, as we're asked to do when The Empress card is displayed.

Angel Number

The Empress (Card 3) is very much like an ascended master, taking the wisdom she's garnered in her life and creating great things with it. (We can choose to work with ascended masters such as Quan-Yin, Buddha, or Jesus.) The number 3 is also connected to creativity, innovation, and communication.

Archangel

Archangel Gabriel is usually mentioned in roles involving communication, such as announcing a birth or being considered a messenger between God and humankind. Her name means "the strength of God," and she's often portrayed carrying a great trumpet to awaken those who slumber and call them to action. She's known for appearing in copper colors.

Astrology

The Empress is associated with the planet Venus in astrology, which represents both emotional and material concerns. It can reflect the aspects in our lives where we have love of a romantic nature or of family, but also the desire to possess lovely things. It's also known to be the planet that influences our creative endeavors—such as art, music, and writing.

~

4

The Emperor
Archangel Michael

*Organization and logic.
Structure and discipline. Leadership.*

The Emperor

The Emperor shows up to tell us that we need a few rules and some organization. By implementing a little structure around our plans, we'll find it easier to bring our dreams to life in the way we intend.

This card represents the constructs of society that make our daily lives possible—such as homes, roads, and infrastructure. The Emperor card is about leadership and integrity; and it can also reflect father figures, people in authority, government officials, and those who are enlisted in the military.

The Dreamer's Journey

Thanks to The Empress, we're excited and ready to make a difference. However, we'll need a plan, and The Emperor is just the person we need to help us put one together. Under his tutelage, we come to understand the power of logic and discipline as a way to bring our creative dreams to life.

His energy feels like a loving but strict father who only wishes to see us succeed and be happy. We also learn from The Emperor that we must consider the needs of others, and not just our own desires, as we move through life.

Symbolism

While The Empress dwells outside in the fertile energy of nature, The Emperor resides indoors. A building is a creation of humankind and therefore represents the structure of society.

Through the open window behind The Emperor, we see the lights of the city he has created. This symbolizes civilization, order, and the things we need to feel safe, such as a roof over our heads.

Our Emperor wears a golden crown and holds a golden scepter. Gold is the metal of royalty.

Swords symbolize many things, including maintaining justice. The Emperor has the sword of Michael to show that he creates with fairness. The sword is not currently drawn, though, because The Emperor has built things so well that he largely focuses on ruling rather than law and order. However, the sword is always accessible should it be needed.

At his feet, we've placed a lute, as we wanted to soften the energy of pure logic that is traditional to the card. Even the Emperor, with his desire for discipline and order, is served by sometimes going to his softer side to soothe his heart with music and art.

Angel Number

The Emperor is Card 4. This number has a long-standing association with angels and their desire to serve, assist, protect, and create opportunities for our growth and success. The number 4 is also about stability, structure, and getting things done.

Archangel

The angel chosen for The Emperor is Archangel Michael, whose name means "he who is like God." This powerful archangel is strong and protective, and like The Emperor, is associated with those who look after our safety (such as the police). He can help us activate the parts of our minds that are about structure and logic. Archangel Michael can help us feel safe and secure, which is another purpose of the Emperor. He resonates to the colors of royal blue and gold.

Astrology

The astrology of this card is Aries. This first sign of the zodiac is direct, independent, assertive, self-assured, and known for taking charge and getting things done. A true go-getter, this sign is always ready to kick-start a project. Sometimes Aries is a better leader than an actual doer, but its commitment to the quest is unquestionable.

∼

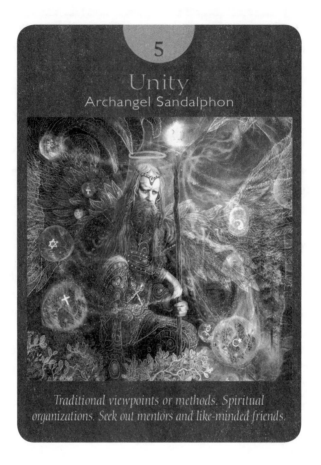

Unity

The Unity card asks us to consider the broader implications of our actions. It's also a duality card. When this card shows up, we may find ourselves being called upon to take a traditional route and do things via tried-and-true methodologies. Or we may be asked to buck tradition by thinking outside the box and doing things our own way. The way to know which message is being presented by Unity is by interpreting the other cards that surround it or, as always, by listening to our intuition.

The Unity card asks us to spend time with like-minded individuals who can help us develop our spiritual gifts. We may feel called upon to join spiritual institutions or schools where we can grow along with others who feel the way we do.

Unity can also indicate that certain rules that have been imposed upon us by society or family no longer serve us. These constraints should be cast off in favor of new guidelines that lead us forward on the path we wish to follow.

The Dreamer's Journey

As humans, we have a tendency to make rules, but what are rules without morality? The Unity card represents a guru or teacher who can help us see the meaning behind our purpose. His wisdom provides us with different guidance from that of those we've met on our journey so far. The mentor on the Unity card challenges us to understand ourselves more deeply. We may know in our hearts that we want to pursue a career as a writer, for example, but *why* do we want that? We may have a plan to change the world, but *how* does our plan benefit the greater good? These are questions of profound meaning and deep spirituality.

Unity doesn't judge our answers per se, but merely gives us access to them, helping us grasp what we label as "good" or "bad," and how that correlates to the world at large. This is a search for the meaning of life that not only enriches our souls, but brings light to those around us.

Symbolism

In traditional tarot, this card is called The Hierophant, and it displays many Christian-based religious icons. In fact, in some of the earliest decks, this card is even called The Pope. In redesigning the card, imagery was chosen that would reflect a broader set of spiritual philosophies.

Seven orbs representing various belief systems fly around Archangel Sandalphon. And while it wasn't possible to place every single belief system on the card, the energy is meant to be all-inclusive. Seven orbs were chosen because that number reflects being on the right path and being spiritually aware.

Above all the orbs is the one true light of Heaven at the top of the archangel's staff.

Around Sandalphon's waist is a set of crossed keys, silver and gold. They represent the conscious and the subconscious.

Angel Number

The Unity card is number 5. If you were going to limit the meaning of this number to one word, it would be *change*! It's all about freedom of ideas and endless curiosity—someone eager to see what's next in life. This number also likes the company of others very much, as it can learn so much about the positive changes they might create for themselves.

Archangel

The archangel for this card is Sandalphon, who's known for delivering prayers from Earth to Heaven. He carries our desires to a loving and benevolent Universe. Sandalphon helps those who are seeking to enrich their inner world, and also helps them find others who are also searching. His halo is a beautiful turquoise.

Astrology

The astrology of this card is Taurus, a sign of determination and faith, and a stable and loyal energy that displays great wisdom and knowledge. It is reliable, and very much values peace. However, this sign can also be a bit rigid in how it sees things. This matches the Unity card's duality message of either sticking with *or* bucking tradition.

～

Intimate relationships. Carefully weigh your decisions. Good health.

The Lovers

When The Lovers card turns up in a reading, of course the first thought may be that a powerful and long-lasting romantic relationship is on its way—and often that *is* the case. This is not the type of love that just falls into our lives for a brief time and then fades away. The Lovers card is a herald of true and enduring love, so engagement or marriage is indicated. If there's a card in tarot that represents a soul mate, then The Lovers card is surely the one. Whether or not the relationship lasts our entire lives, we will absolutely be changed forever.

This card can also signify an important decision. When that occurs in a reading, we're encouraged to make a choice of the heart. We must *feel* the right direction to take. With the presence of Archangel Raphael, this card can also indicate a return to health.

The Dreamer's Journey

As we continue along our path, we discover The Lovers. With this card, we're either reminded of the influence that a heart-to-heart connection with another person can have over us, or we discover it for the first time. We come to realize the power and importance that emotion can play in our lives. In the story of this journey, this is where The Dreamer learns of romantic love for the first time. Of course, that's a metaphor, so this experience is attributed to us or our clients in a reading. The relationship we encounter with this card can also be a very intimate, yet platonic one. If so, it probably involves a companion whose friendship will last a lifetime.

Our hearts themselves tell us that our choices can also be guided by our emotions. It's not just the cool logic of The Emperor or the morality of the Unity card that can lead us in the right direction. Sometimes the heart must be our only compass.

Symbolism

This card represents opposites: the feminine and the masculine.

Behind the woman is a tree with five fruits to represent the five senses, which are based on information the body takes in. Behind the man is a tree with fruit to represent the signs of the zodiac. At the time tarot was created, astrology was considered purely a science. Therefore, it can be said that the woman's perception is all feeling, while the man's is intellectual.

The man's attention is focused toward the woman and her role in his life, which is a very worldly concern. The woman's focus is on Archangel Raphael, representing a desire for the spiritual.

But there's true love to be found in the successful commingling of our experience as humans with the knowledge that we're also children of the Divine.

Their differences also remind us that, regardless of the genders of the people involved, opposites attract, as they help us learn and grow.

In the foreground, marigolds are growing. These flowers are associated with healing, and therefore with Archangel Raphael.

Violets are also in the image, representing fidelity and love.

Angel Number

The Lovers card is number 6 in tarot. This is a number that's focused on worldly concerns such as fertility and carrying on the family line. In traditional numerology, the number 6 reflects caring, love, understanding, and nurturing. It represents a true and unfaltering concern for family and for others we love.

Archangel

Archangel Raphael is known for heralding love in ancient texts. Therefore, his place in The Lovers card is particularly appropriate. Raphael's name means "God heals," and he's also considered to be the healing archangel that we can call upon for any concerns regarding health. He presents himself in beautiful emerald green.

Astrology

The Lovers card is ruled by Gemini, the sign of communication, but also of duality. The same principles of light and dark, masculine and feminine, are present in this astrological sign. It is yin and yang, and just like The Lovers card, it is the mix of these two energies that makes it so amazing.

$\sim$

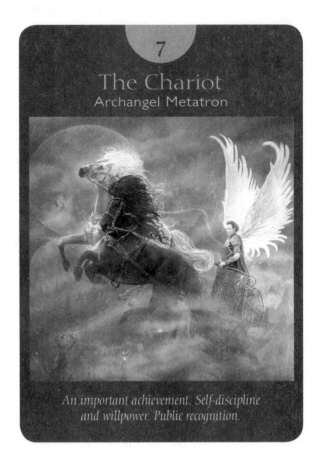

The Chariot

The Chariot is the card that refers to heading out on a big adventure. We may deal with many situations that we've never encountered before, so sometimes it's necessary to attempt to simultaneously make more than one person happy. We may have to juggle priorities in such a way that all of these obligations are fulfilled. The Chariot is a card that's all about the balancing of opposing forces. We discover something new and then try to accomplish great things for the first time. This mastering of many things at once is done via the mind, a dedicated purpose, and sheer will.

The Chariot is a card of success, so it can indicate an upcoming promotion, job offer, or award. This card often asks us to feel safe when promoting ourselves or our endeavors in the media. Obviously, it can also symbolize modes of transportation such as cars, planes, or trains.

The Dreamer's Journey

Next on our voyage we encounter The Chariot. All the cards along the journey so far have led us to this moment. We've taken our leap of faith; have become clear on what we wish to accomplish; and have created a plan that includes logic, morality, and heart. Now we head out into the world to put all of that to the test.

With The Chariot, we discover that life is challenging. There are always people to please, multiple considerations to balance, and many moving parts to our chariot that must be maintained. Here, we discover that there's a *power* in merely desiring that our endeavors be a success; we learn self-discipline and determination.

The charioteer is generally seen as having been victorious on his quest—so much so that the accolades thrown his way make him very visible in the public eye. For some, the joy of that is natural, and it requires no effort beyond accepting it and simply taking a bow. For others, that type of acknowledgment can feel very uncomfortable. The Chariot teaches us to have pride in our accomplishments and to allow others to express their appreciation in a public way.

Symbolism

Metatron rides his chariot pulled by two horses: one black, one white. These are competing forces that The Chariot rider is so masterfully keeping in perfect balance.

His reins aren't real, but made of energy to symbolize his ability to use pure desire to keep these raucous forces working together.

On the side of the chariot is the *merkabah,* otherwise known as "Metatron's Cube." This magical creation is called the "chariot of God" and is a symbol of sacred geometry. We can focus on this image to help us manifest anything we're trying to create.

Angel Number

The Chariot is Card 7. This is a number of single-mindedness and purpose that seeks out the *truth* in every situation. A very spiritual number, it fits in well with the concept of a human who ascends to the realm of archangel and then rides a magical chariot to Heaven. Clearly, Metatron is following his life path perfectly!

Archangel

The archangel on this card is Metatron, returning for a second appearance. He was chosen because he's one of two archangels who were once human. He was said to have so pleased God that he rode to Heaven in a chariot of fire. Metatron can also help recharge our batteries so that we have the energy necessary to fulfill our goals. His colors are green and violet, or dark pink.

Astrology

The astrology for this card is Cancer. While this is a very watery sign for such an action-filled card, keep in mind that Cancers are greatly concerned with security and being in control. Cancers are tenacious and very adaptable, which helps them maintain a mastery over any situation that assures success.

$\sim$

8

Justice
Archangel Raguel

*Fair and just decisions. Do what you
know is right. Stand up for your beliefs.*

Justice

The Justice card encourages us to always do what we know
is right—and in doing so, we can know that justice is always on
our side. If we find ourselves in a situation where someone has
the ability to make a judgment or evaluation in our favor or not,
drawing the Justice card is a very good indication that things will
go our way, but legal contracts should be reviewed very carefully
before signing.

Justice also asks us to stand up for our beliefs—to know that
we're right, and to hold firm to our convictions.

As mentioned in Chapter 2, Justice was originally Card 8 in tarot until the Rider-Waite deck flipped its position with the Strength card in 1909. I've chosen to return it to its original position in the *Angel Tarot Cards* in order to restore the continuity of The Dreamer's Journey.

The Dreamer's Journey

When we make decisions or interact with others, we're accountable for our actions. As we visit the Justice card along our journey, we learn the rules of life, both karmic and judicial. The choices that we made along our path were put into action with The Chariot, and now those actions may be reviewed by others. Justice looks at the way we treated those around us as we moved forward. If we were kind and fair to everyone and acted with integrity, then Justice will be proud of our growth and will defend us. With this card, we're taught to stand up for ourselves when we know that we're right.

Justice also asks us to be activists in our own ways. If we see injustice or unkindness in the world, we're asked to call attention to it. Each of us has concerns that touch our hearts, and we need not try to change *everything* in the world. If we all were to pursue the causes that mean the most to us, then the world's inequalities would be resolved!

Symbolism

Archangel Raguel floats before two pillars that give the appearance of belonging to a court of law.

He carries perfectly balanced scales to show fairness and objective choices.

He also carries an upright sword. This shows us that justice is double-edged. On one side, it makes fair and just decisions. On the other side, it expects accountability, demanding that we remain in our highest integrity.

Angel Number

Justice is Card 8. This number is often considered to be related to material prosperity and abundance, and that's true. However, the very shape of the number shows an even structure of two natures. It has an understanding of right and wrong, black and white, light and dark. This number is committed to karmic balancing.

Archangel

The archangel here is Raguel. He's known for being the angel we can call on when we find ourselves in a challenging situation with another person. He softens the energy and brings about reconciliation and compromise—perfect for Justice! Raguel's halo is pale blue.

Astrology

The astrology for this card is Libra, which is usually represented by the scales found on this card. This sign is open-minded, balanced, idealistic, and very focused on what is fair.

∼

The Hermit

This card is very much about mentoring or being mentored, especially with respect to spiritual teachings. We may be called upon to seek out a teacher to help us move forward, or perhaps we've done enough inner exploration that we have great insights to share with others.

The Hermit asks us to go within to pursue self-discovery. He compels us to be quiet and listen to the small, still voice that comes from the depths of our souls.

This card can indicate getting good advice from someone wise, and can also encourage us to take some quiet time to reevaluate our plans.

The Dreamer's Journey

Everyone needs an occasional time-out, a moment to be with oneself and reflect. And so it is with The Hermit.

Or is it?

You see, the little-known secret about The Hermit is that he's not nearly as solitary as he appears. He stands at the top of the mountain holding out his lantern for those who are climbing up behind him. Just out of view, his students are rising to join him. He shines his light so that the seekers of truth can find him.

As Dreamers, we find ourselves needing time to assimilate all that we've learned up to this point on the journey. We ask ourselves questions such as, "Am I on the right path?" or "Is the effort I'm putting into this endeavor really worth it?" Answers to those questions come from within, or from a spiritual teacher like The Hermit, who can guide us to our own conclusions.

Symbolism

The Hermit stands at the top of a mountain to represent that he's risen to new spiritual heights. What better vantage point from which to see the world and our place in it?

He carries a cane for support to show that it's all right to rely on others when necessary.

His lantern symbolizes that he's been enlightened by many of his experiences so far.

From the lantern, fireflies (which represent our inner light) zoom around. They show that this light can fly off to other places and illuminate other souls. Fireflies are also a sign that there's a great deal of magic in the world.

While this card is associated with Virgo (see the Astrology section below), The Hermit stands with Saturn behind him. In astrology, a "Saturn return" occurs in our birth charts about every 28 years. During that time, people often feel the need to reflect on their lives to date. If your clients pull this card, they may be in for a time of inner exploration.

Angel Number

The number 9 symbolizes humanitarianism, both in traditional numerology and in angel numbers. Just like The Hermit, who is also a humanitarian and working to bring light into the world, there's a certain amount of self-sacrifice associated with it. For example, with the number 971, we know right away that numerologically it's going to reduce to 8, the sum of the other two numbers ($9 + 7 + 1 = 17$, $1 + 7 = 8$). The 9 in a sense "sacrifices" itself. That's what makes it the perfect number for The Hermit. But even outside of mathematics, 9 is the number that says "Get to work, Lightworkers! The world needs you to fully commit to your life purpose."

Archangel

Our grand old wizard Archangel Raziel has returned, ready to teach us the secrets that he's learned. He has moved past The Magician card that's indicative of the ability to create. Now the question is: *Why* should we create? How can we help the world with our magical abilities?

Raziel appears to us in rainbow colors.

Astrology

This card resonates to the energy of hardworking, diligent, devoted, and nurturing Virgo. Much like our Hermit, this sign is extremely dedicated to helping others, having learned the perfect way to accomplish its goals. As such, it wants to share that information with its apprentices. Virgo is very studious and wants to know the "whys" and "hows" of every situation.

⁓

A time of positive change. A situation suddenly moves forward. Fortune is on your side!

The Wheel

The Wheel is a card of luck. For those of us who know astrology, this card is linked to Jupiter, so our experience with it is that it's most often *good* luck. It's also a card of renewed movement, so while we may have taken a little time to rest and reflect with The Hermit, we're now back on our path. The pause is over, and delays are a thing of the past.

However, if The Wheel is surrounded by challenging cards, or falls in a position of the past, it can sometimes indicate that our opportunities have become limited. The Wheel does have a certain attachment to karma, so when it spins, it's often because our own actions have set it into motion.

The Dreamer's Journey

Well, it's been great spending time with The Hermit. We discovered a new sense of balance as well as the answers we were seeking. However, now it's time to move forward, and sure enough, that's the message of The Wheel. There should be a reward for spending time in a state of spiritual growth, and now we've found a bit of good luck. There may be a "happy accident" that sets us back into action, or perhaps we're just ready to get going. It's true that a wheel turns in both directions, but the forward motion of our journey tends to set us in a positive direction. We *are* the masters of our own fate, after all.

Symbolism

Archangel Michael sits inside a wheel of the zodiac to show us that life is ever-changing. We move through life just like Mother Earth moves through the seasons, and the stars move through the sky.

The four elemental icons—Fire, Water, Earth and Air—are depicted on this card. They were also shown on the belt of The Magician and represent the elements at our disposal to control our own destinies.

While in traditional tarot, this card has a sense of fate about it, in truth everyone has free will. We can change the direction of our lives if we so desire.

These elements and their attachment to both The Magician and The Wheel cards show that we have the resources necessary to make those changes.

Angel Number

The number 10 carries with it a sense of good luck. It's a 1 (which can be a beginning), coupled with the God number of 0. It often means a change of luck in our favor. Because 1 + 0 still equals 1, it's very important to see the changes that the wheel brings as positive and designed for our benefit. After all, perception becomes reality.

Archangel

Archangel Michael returns in this card. As the archangel who helps us with life-purpose issues, he can assist us in making the changes we desire, especially if we feel that our lives have stopped moving forward and we need help to get going again.

His colors are deep royal blue and gold.

Astrology

As mentioned, the astrology of this card is lucky old Jupiter. It's expansive, positive, and optimistic. That is why we usually find that this card indicates good luck. Jupiter has only the best intentions for us and wants us to learn, grow, and be all that we can be.

∼

Strength

The Strength card is about exercising the desires of our will in a way where no one is harmed. This card is named for the type of firm resolve where we go within and find that our baser instincts have been tamed. And with that taming, we become stronger.

Often for true kindness to come forth, we must find it within ourselves to forgive. We're asked to let go of any judgment of ourselves or others, and view those around us with forgiveness and tolerance.

As mentioned in Chapter 2, Strength was Card 11 in tarot for centuries until the Rider-Waite deck flipped its position with the Justice card in 1909. In order to keep the intended flow of The Dreamer's Journey intact, I chose to return it to its original position in the *Angel Tarot Cards.*

The Dreamer's Journey

In our journey as The Dreamer, we learned all about the power of control and sheer will with The Chariot. However, the time we spent with The Hermit has put us in touch with our more spiritual side. We've discovered that there's another way to power our dream besides pure determination. We can do it with kindness. The exercising of compassion is a critical aspect on our journey of enlightenment. With the Strength card, we discover a very beautiful woman working in concert with a tiger—one of nature's most powerful animals. Her kindness toward the tiger has brought her cooperation that she could never have attained with brute force.

Doves of peace fly ahead of this duo as they move farther along in their adventure. The lady and the tiger will need patience, since they're only halfway through their journey.

Symbolism

Archangel Ariel rides a tiger, a symbol of great strength and courage. However, the tiger is her ally, not her servant.

Tigers are known for their great power, yet this one is content to work with Archangel Ariel due to her love of nature. Beauty and angelic wisdom move in concert with the power and soulfulness of the animal kingdom.

Behind Ariel a city glows, although they're clearly moving out into the forest. In this card, the comforts of civilization live in harmony with the wilds of nature.

Archangel Ariel carries a shield that has a dove with the symbol of infinity in its beak, while other doves fly about. Doves represent peace, and the infinity sign tells us that there's no end to the peace we can create.

The doves paired with the tiger also tell us that true strength is wielded in peace.

The flowers are Stars of Bethlehem and are said to bring hope. They're also sometimes given to someone as a way to say "I'm sorry."

Angel Number

Strength is Card 11, and is considered a "master number." Due to this number's deep connection with inner wisdom, it's able to manifest amazing things, thus bringing with it an obligation to remain in a positive and uplifting energy. This number is also connected with great spiritual insights and often implies a sense of responsibility that encourages acting in ways that display a purity of conscience.

Archangel

Archangel Ariel's name means "lioness of God." She's also the archangel most closely associated with nature and animals. She works in tandem with Archangel Raphael in the healing of animals and is a favorite of environmentalists. She's known for her ability to manifest the material needs of those who call upon her.

Her color is pale pink.

Astrology

Astrologically, this card is Leo, a sign that is loving, ambitious, powerful, and loyal. And, of course, Leo has a flair for the dramatic (like taking a ride on a tiger). Leo is also very idealistic and broad-minded, which allows this sign to see others without feeling the need to judge their path. Leo is very humane in its viewpoint of the world, which is in line with Archangel Ariel and the way she sees planet Earth and all its inhabitants.

~

Awakening

When this card shows up, there may be a temporary pause in the action while we reflect on where we wish to go next, but it's only that . . . temporary. The action picks back up once we've had our Awakening. In the meantime, this is a good time to review our plans to make sure that what we've learned to date hasn't created a need to change our strategies for success.

Awakening could be said to be a quirky card—an archangel flying upside down with a trumpet in hand. But there's a reason for this imagery, and it's to celebrate our own uniqueness. When the Awakening card comes into a reading, look for aspects in which clients may be trying to "fit in" with those around them. The truth is, their purpose would be better served if they just let that idea go and showed the world who they really are. (Even if that's pretty quirky, too!)

The Dreamer's Journey

As we move forward on the journey of our lives, invariably our viewpoints adapt and change to match our experiences. We come to see the world differently (and the world certainly looks very different to us when we're upside down!). Perhaps we come to see that we don't like things the way they are, so we choose to change the way we're living. Those changes may be unexpected, and our solutions to the challenges they create can be quite unusual with this card, as it also asks us to express our uniqueness and to be as eclectic and original as we can be. We may be called upon to spring into action, or perhaps we find that we're just going to have to wait patiently for Heaven's plans for us to unfold.

Symbolism

Archangel Gabriel swoops down from Heaven with her trumpet. She's associated with this instrument due to her history as a communicator of important announcements. A trumpet has long been a symbol for waking people up from their sleep or daydreams.

Beyond Gabriel, the view is hazy. It's difficult to see what's around her, which signifies that we may not be seeing things clearly when we draw this card.

Like the traditional imagery for this card, Gabriel's upside-down vantage point offers a new perspective on what's happening.

On her dress, Gabriel wears the symbol of Neptune, the astrological association for this card.

Angel Number

The number 12 is quite magical. There are 12 astrological signs, 12 houses of the zodiac, and 12 months of the year. There are many references in spirituality and religion to the number 12. The Awakening card brings with it revelation and inspiration. Indeed, its message tries to make us aware that our path may need to take a new turn, and the way we perceive our situation will have a powerful effect on how it unfolds.

Archangel

This is the second appearance of beautiful Archangel Gabriel, dressed in her color of copper. Since she's known for being the angel of messages, I thought it perfectly appropriate that if someone were to sound a trumpet blast of epiphany, it should be Gabriel!

Astrology

Astrologically, this card is Neptune, a very dreamy sign with an amazing imagination. It's easy to fall asleep to our situation within the energy of Neptune, as it's also very sensitive. When it's time to become more aware of the way we live, and to envision something new, Neptune is the perfect energy.

~

Release

Perhaps the most misunderstood card of the Major Arcana, Release was traditionally called Death in tarot. And yet, it didn't refer to a physical death at all, but rather, an ending. A reading with Release in the spread indicates that clients are in a situation that's no longer serving them, and it's time to move on.

With Release, it's best to take our time moving through the changes that are before us. Reaching out to friends or family is a wise way to deal with what may feel like a loss. It's also an excellent time to face our fears so that we can be in complete control of our future.

The Release card often brings with it great spiritual insights and personal transformation.

The Dreamer's Journey

As a result of our time with the Awakening card, we've become more aware of changes that need to be made. Those changes may very well mean initiating some endings in order to complete the current cycle. There may be transitions that we welcome and have brought about of our own free will, and we may even be relieved. Or there may be sadness in the completion that we have to work through.

Now, of course, with endings come new beginnings, and so it is with the Release card. What makes Release different from other cards in tarot that refer to endings is that we're asked to stand in the moment and experience it. In order to grow, we mustn't just rush past this situation. There's great emotional and spiritual enlightenment to be had, as long as we take the time to smell those white roses along the path.

Symbolism

Archangel Azrael stands with arms outstretched, ready to embrace us.

On his robe is a phoenix, the bird that is forever reborn, as we will be reborn from our challenges.

He walks through a field of white roses, symbolizing purity of intention, but they're also a symbol of rebirth.

In the background, a white horse comforts her young. Horses have many symbolic meanings, but among them is the freedom to move on to other places.

The two towers in the background connect this card to both The High Priestess and The Moon to indicate that in this time of release, all has been revealed. The spiritual insights and meditations of The High Priestess helped put us on the path that led us to where we are now. Later on, we'll see how The Moon card brings further revelations.

Angel Number

The number 13 is considered a karmic number. Many view it as unlucky, but that's simply not true. What is more often the case is that this number brings with it a time of change and transformation in our lives. It's a number that's also associated with ascended masters, such as Jesus, Quan-Yin, and Buddha, who are willing to guide us to a new and much happier life.

Archangel

Azrael is the most elegant and tender of all the archangels. He comes with the power of the grace of the Divine to comfort us and walk with us through any challenging times. His name means "whom God helps," and his color is creamy white.

Astrology

Astrologically, this card is connected to Scorpio, a sign that is very adept at new beginnings and embracing endings. It's also the sign of the zodiac most closely associated with deep inner exploration and evaluation.

~

The need for balance and moderation.
Cooperation and compromise. Wait for perfect timing.

Balance

Balance was traditionally called Temperance in tarot. This is a word that means to *meld* or *combine*. I felt that renaming the card Balance made it much easier to understand for both reader and client. Balance refers to a time of cooperation with others, and may ask us to be willing to compromise our plans just a bit so that everyone can be successful. The blending of ideas is sure to bring about greater success.

This card asks us for patience; if things aren't working the way we're hoping, it may just be an issue of timing. When we contemplate major changes in our lives, this card asks us to take it slow and easy and to think things through carefully. This is not a time for acting impulsively!

The Dreamer's Journey

Once we come to the Balance card, we've moved through a time of revelation and change. Now we must integrate those epiphanies into our lives. We have the opportunity to rise to a higher consciousness and are moving forward down the path to enlightenment. However, that path is more of a stroll than a race. Clearly, the archangel on the card is not in any hurry.

Life is a constant mixing and balancing of experiences that affect our future. We never stop learning, but we may have to repeat certain types of events in our lives if we forget to pause and understand their meaning.

Symbolism

Archangel Zadkiel holds two goblets from which he pours water back and forth. He is eternally blending the knowledge gained from his experiences.

He has one foot on the earth and the other in the water. Earth represents our outer perceptions, while the water symbolizes our inner wisdom. This card shows that these two worlds are coming together in order to create something amazing.

The irises are named for the goddess Iris, who was known as the messenger of the gods and also the goddess of the rainbow. In ancient Hebrew, the word for *rainbow* was the same as the word for *Sagittarius,* thereby giving us a very visual cue as to the card's astrological association.

Zadkiel wears a triangle within a square on his waist. This represents spirit held within matter, just as *we* are spirit held within material bodies.

Angel Number

The number 14 is another karmic number. It is one of balance and peaceful coexistence with others. It can also be a bit restless, and therefore needs to evaluate choices carefully. It has a very positive connection with angels that helps it keep that hopeful viewpoint that's also indicated by the Balance card's optimistic outlook.

Archangel

Archangel Zadkiel's name means "the righteousness of God." He's known for being helpful to anyone who's in a time of learning (especially students). When we find ourselves at an important juncture in our lives, Zadkiel can help us remember where we've been before and accurately assess where we'd like to go next.

He's an archangel of healing who comes to us in the color of deep indigo blue.

Astrology

This card is represented by Sagittarius, a sign of spiritual understanding and optimism even when it's been through adversity. Sagittarius is blessed with great faith and hope. It's also a mutable sign of the zodiac, which means that it has the ability to easily adapt to any situation and relate to almost any person. It's difficult to feel down when the energy of Sagittarius is present!

~

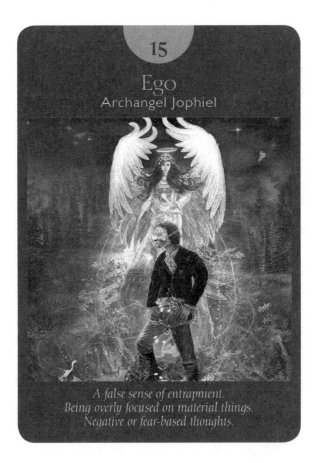

Ego

The Ego card reflects situations (usually of our own making) where we feel trapped. It seems as though our path has become completely hidden, and it feels like there's no way forward. Of course, this is an illusion. We aren't really as stuck as we think we are, and freedom comes with a change of our thoughts from pessimism to optimism.

Ego can also reveal other significant challenges, such as addiction or dependency, that can hold us back from happiness. As such, this is a very important card in tarot, since it can give us insight into our clients' or family members' challenges with substance use.

This card sometimes refers to someone who's too focused on material or worldly things, and therefore might indicate excessive debt. It can also signify those who aren't taking responsibility for their actions or choices.

The Dreamer's Journey

Our next stop on the path of The Dreamer's Journey is the need to deal with our human egos. It's an indicator that we may not have a clear view of ourselves or our motives. We may be confused by what feels like limitations that we can't get past, but in reality, these confinements are our own creations. What makes this card so powerful and helpful is that once we realize that our entrapments are self-made, we can then see that we must also have the power to free ourselves.

When we allow our egos to take over, we often find ourselves making choices that are based on fear or negative thinking. This hinders our progress and can create self-fulfilling prophecies that we'd be better off without. It's also a reminder that our focus on daily life and our acquisition of "things" may not be what really matters right now. Perhaps it's time to review our priorities!

Symbolism

The Dreamer has experienced a bit of a detour he didn't mean to take, and finds himself chained and unable to move.

His chains are attached to a pot of gold to represent that he's bound to his material concerns and the worldly fears of those around him.

He wears a mask that blinds his vision, to symbolize that in his current state, he can't really see where he's headed or how very off course he is.

A butterfly, a symbol of evolution, zips past to remind us that moving past our current shortcomings is completely within our power.

The crane is a symbol of spiritual enlightenment. This one has followed The Dreamer into his predicament to remind him of his ability to change his life. It's always possible to make course corrections in order to match the life purpose we came to Earth to accomplish.

Archangel Jophiel has come to guide The Dreamer out of his nonspiritual focus and lead him back to a place of happiness and fulfillment.

Angel Number

The number 15 can be very fortuitous, drawing in prosperity and abundance. However, it can also be a number that's very sensitive to criticism. Harsh words from others can create a negative self-perception that can be difficult to escape. Of course, anyone can change; we all have free will. Staying positive and taking the steps necessary to improve our lives can help us get free and clear of the Ego card.

Archangel

Archangel Jophiel's name means "beauty of God." When our thoughts have fallen into negativity or pessimism, she can help us rise above it to regain our optimism and see our way clear to freedom. When we've lost our way, Jophiel reminds us just how beautiful life can be.

Her color is a dark pink, and her presence is often associated with the scent of roses.

Astrology

Astrologically, this card is Capricorn, a very responsible, practical, and competent sign that often deals with business. Because it has a deep desire to build something of importance, it can be associated with overworking and/or being very focused on making money.

~

16

Life Experience
Archangel Chamuel

A significant life event. A powerful revelation that leads to change. Time to spread your wings.

Life Experience

When this card shows up in a reading, it's trying to tell us that we need to break out of old, outdated, and confining boundaries. This may occur because we've become aware of our situation and therefore choose to break free of our own accord. Or it may happen when a particular life event brings us an awareness that we can't deny.

In traditional tarot, this card was called The Tower and could be misunderstood; therefore, I renamed it Life Experience. Many had associated this card with frightening things happening. However, getting married is a life experience. Having a baby is a life experience. Graduating from college is a life experience. All of these events undeniably change the way we live on a daily basis and bring about a new awareness.

Often this card can represent an amazing revelation that helps us understand where we are in life versus where we'd like to be. This epiphany is one of freedom and of seeing things clearly—perhaps for the first time.

The Dreamer's Journey

The mask of the Ego card has been removed, and now we can *see*. However, just because we can see the path laid out before us, that doesn't mean we'll walk down it. Human beings can be incredibly resistant to change. Our angels may wish us to go happily along this path, but sometimes we don't get the message (or pretend we don't). That's when Heaven may step in to give us a little push.

But even when Heaven does lend a hand in sending us down a new path, we must remember that The Dreamer's Journey is one of joy and enlightenment. If Life Experience brings change into our lives, it will inevitably take us in a direction that we'll be glad we followed.

Symbolism

In the background of this card is a tower that represents the life we previously created.

We're being led away from it, down a new garden path, by Archangel Chamuel, who's known for being able to see that which may be invisible to us.

The skies are a bit cloudy and dark where we've come from, but we can see the dawn breaking through in the direction we're now headed.

In front of Archangel Chamuel flies a cuckoo bird, which is symbolic of great life changes.

Butterflies further remind us of our ability to evolve and change no matter what life throws at us.

The hourglass in the foreground tells us that the time has come to make the changes we know in our hearts we must make. It's also a reminder that if we don't make these changes, then the Heavenly push that was just mentioned may be on its way.

Angel Number

The number 16 is karmic in nature and speaks of restlessness, or challenges in our lives that compel us to make changes. This number drives us to seek a deep purpose in our lives. While making these changes, it's important that we stay positive.

Archangel

Archangel Chamuel's name means "he who sees God." There's nothing beyond his vision. He can always help us find what we're looking for—whether it's a new career, a romantic partner, or a better understanding of the truth of our situation.

His color is pale green.

Astrology

This card is associated with Mars, a planet that's bold, courageous, and daring. Mars is always ready to take a chance or head out on a new quest. This passionate planet encourages us to be the very best that we can be, to accomplish all we can, and to fulfill our life purpose. If we're feeling confined by our situation, Mars can help us break out of whatever is constraining us.

~

The Star

The Star card is one of unending hope, pure faith, and true understanding. It indicates that our choices have been such that we can begin to make longer-term plans. We have a sense of purpose that allows us to see that an abundant future is within our reach. If I were to limit this card's definition to just one word, it would be *faith*.

When we see this card, we also consider it a "make a wish" type of card. Since we're on the right path when it's drawn, and long-term plans seem certain, why not wish for what we want?

The Dreamer's Journey

Our journey has taken us through many challenges and opportunities for growth. The Star card tells us that now we can enjoy the happiness that comes from the spiritual work we've done. We've let go of the past, cast off the chains of our egos, and made the changes we needed to make. We're now free to set off on a new level of prosperity and freedom!

However, just as those mountains in the image are far off in the distance, we're also asked to make our plans from the perspective of the big picture. At this point, we should be visualizing our lives as we would like them to be in the long run as opposed to just next week.

Symbolism

Archangel Jophiel pours out water from two urns. She has no worries that the water will run out, as the source is eternal and unlimited. She has total faith that her path is perfect.

The water pouring out also symbolizes the power of meditation.

One urn pours out water that falls into five streams, representing the five senses, which are enhanced by meditation.

The water then falls into a pool below that represents the universal consciousness.

In the sky are seven stars, reflecting the seven chakras.

The mountains in the background indicate the great heights that we can aspire to at this time in our lives.

Angel Number

The number for The Star is 17, which carries with it good fortune. Much of that comes as a result of the positive energy we've put out into the Universe that has now returned to reward us. Our insights when under the energy of number 17 are accurate and precise.

Archangel

Jophiel returns in her very natural role as the archangel who shows us how beautiful life can be. Her positive energy helps us keep the faith that The Star card represents. We can ask her to help us remain in a positive mind-set while we plan our joyful new future.

As stated before, her color is dark pink.

Astrology

This card is ruled by friendly, future-minded, and humanitarian-focused Aquarius. This is a visionary sign that can see the possibilities of the future—not just for ourselves, but for *all* of humankind.

∼

The Moon

The Moon card asks us to be awake to the intuitive insights that present themselves in order to provide clarity with respect to our situation. Psychic visions as well as our nighttime dreams should be given great credence. What is our subconscious trying to tell us? Could there be more going on here than meets the eye?

The Moon card can refer to times in our lives when we feel insecure or uncertain. However, these are usually irrational fears or unnecessary worries. Just as the real Moon reflects light upon us at night, so does this card indicate that the light of truth will be revealed to us.

The Dreamer's Journey

Now we come to The Moon card. Archangel Haniel returns after her previous appearance as The High Priestess. Indeed, there are common attributes shared by The High Priestess and The Moon. Both are very intuitive, and both have something to say about what was once unknown but which is now within our grasp.

Under the light of this shining Moon, things that we thought weren't possible (or even real) suddenly come to life. There are opportunities for enlightenment that are so wondrous we can scarcely believe it. Fears that have previously held us back can now be released. Chances are that these worries and concerns aren't even valid anymore. Perhaps they never were!

Symbolism

Archangel Haniel stands with two pillars in the background. These are the same ones she stood in front of in The High Priestess card. We've traveled a long way, so here we see the pillars from the other side.

Archangel Haniel still wears the cross of equal proportions she wore in The High Priestess card. Conscious and subconscious thoughts are balanced.

On one side of her is a wolf, on the other side a dog. They represent the wild and the tame. They're the height of nature and the pinnacle of art, and Haniel is the balance between them.

Two streams flow into a central pond—conscious and subconscious knowledge converging.

The pond of water is the same pool of meditation and inner wisdom that we referenced on The Balance card and The Star card.

In traditional tarot, this card usually indicates a very dark night. But just as it's possible to see the Moon during the day, this card can be perceived with a lighter interpretation. We can face our fears and do so in the light!

Angel Number

The Moon is Card 18. Under this number, people may feel compelled to express their concerns or fears. With this number, there's also a connection between the spiritual and material worlds, which may feel at odds with one another. So we must stay positive about our expectations so that our material needs can be met in ways we feel good about.

Archangel

Archangel Haniel returns with all her psychic and intuitive powers to show us the truth of our situation. In her pale blue moonlight colors, she's aware of a type of beauty and poignant knowledge we haven't yet seen. But soon—very soon—we will see what *she* sees.

Astrology

This card is ruled by Pisces, a very psychic, sensitive, and spiritual sign. In astrology, Pisces rules the 12th house of the zodiac— the house of unseen or hidden knowledge. However, Pisces is the most intuitive of the signs and can help us come to know that which has been unknowable up until now.

~

Happy outcome! Brilliant new ideas that lead to success. Have confidence in yourself!

The Sun

Grand epiphanies are possible with The Sun. Incredible ideas with infinite opportunities enter our consciousness where we can act upon them. This card also reflects someone whose self-confidence either has grown or is on the rise.

If we keep our thoughts positive, then there's no way we won't be successful. This card can also represent a return to vibrant physical and emotional health.

The Dreamer's Journey

Our time with The Moon brought us further insights, and now we turn around to see The Sun. Great joy and success are inspired by this card. It shows us that we've evolved, we've grown, and we've created the world we wanted!

With The Sun, we can expect to experience the true joy of life and all the wonderful things it has to offer. As a result, we may receive public recognition for our teachings or accomplishments. Our journey is nearly over, and true enlightenment is within our grasp.

Symbolism

Archangel Uriel stands on a wall that represents humankind's successful ability to adapt to the difficulties of life.

Uriel is backlit by the Sun rising in a new dawn, a joyful new morning that reflects the direction our lives are headed.

Butterflies, the symbol of evolution and growth, swirl around Archangel Uriel, proving that we've come a long way on our journey.

Four sunflowers bloom happily at his feet, representing both the four suits of the Minor Arcana, and the four elements of Fire, Water, Earth, and Air.

Angel Number

The number 19 is the last of the karmic numbers. It's where we come to successful endings and therefore create new beginnings for ourselves. Suddenly, everything becomes crystal clear with this number. We discover that we *do* know our life purpose and that it's time to act upon it. We come to believe in ourselves so that we can move forward with confidence and hope for a beautiful future.

Archangel

Archangel Uriel, whose name means "light of God," heralds the great epiphanies that have brought us to this place of enlightenment and joy. Uriel has the ability to not only bring us great insights, but also bless us with emotional healing.

His beautiful wings and his halo reflect his golden-yellow color.

Astrology

Naturally, the astrological association for this card is the Sun! In astrology, the Sun is our identity, our personality, and our true nature. It also represents creativity and the areas of our lives where we really shine.

~

Renewal

Renewal indicates that we're close to completing an important task. This card asks us to pause and review the past and our achievements so that we can decide where we want to go in the future. This can include career changes we've been pondering, so we must take the time to think through our options very carefully.

We may have big decisions to make, but this card can also assure us that we're ready for any endeavor we've been preparing for. School exams, legal proceedings, or certification tests will go well for us.

The Dreamer's Journey

In original tarot, this card was named Judgment. And while this name and its imagery presented the perception of being judged by someone else, the card has more to do with how we see our own actions than how others perceive them.

Renewal indicates that we've come a very long way and have seen amazing and wonderful things. However, it's now time to pause and review our past so that we can understand where we are and where we want to be. Renewal beckons us to move in a new direction. We feel that we're at a crossroads, and we feel optimistic about any endings that may be near. We have big decisions to make, and we're ready to make them—both emotionally and spiritually.

We hear a calling. We can feel that it's our destiny to continue to do great things . . . and the possibilities are endless!

Symbolism

Archangel Jeremiel stands upon turbulent waters, which represent the challenging experiences that we've had as we've traveled along our journey.

And yet, in the here and now, the water that the family is standing on is completely calm, showing the peace our efforts have manifested.

The man is the conscious, the woman is the subconscious, and the child represents higher consciousness. Together they symbolize a healthy balance of our inner and outer worlds.

Archangel Jeremiel holds a staff with a light on top that's the color of our crown chakra, showing that we've developed self-knowledge and spiritual awareness.

Angel Number

The number 20 signifies great compassion, caring, and affection. This is a number of service to others and to the world. In The Dreamer's Journey, the Renewal card indicates that we've come to a place of evolution and spiritual growth that matches the number 20 in resonance and energy. With this number, we can know that God is helping us with every step we take. Our optimism for the future is completely warranted.

Archangel

Archangel Jeremiel is the angel who helps us evaluate our lives so that we can understand the changes we wish to make in the future. His name means "mercy of God," and his color is dark purple. Just as Source is infinitely loving and merciful, so should we be when reviewing our own lives.

Astrology

Pluto is known as the planet of transformation. When it comes into our world, things are likely to change—and change fairly dramatically. Just like the Renewal card, Pluto comes along to push us to attain greater heights. We can be renewed and reborn so that we can be even *more* than we were in the past.

~

The World

The World indicates moving to the next level in our personal lives or careers. There may be a promotion or a new position that's both challenging and promising in our future. It can reflect moving to a new home or city.

This card is also one of enlightenment. We've followed our own evolution, and we have complete clarity, which provides us with an understanding of where we want to go next.

The Dreamer's Journey

Well, we did it! This is the end of The Dreamer's Journey! We've conquered our egos and found joy. We have mastered all our tasks, have enjoyed great success, and have indeed arrived at the place of peace and happiness from which we entered the world. This card indicates victory, accomplishment, and completion. We need to enjoy this moment!

The World denotes having come full circle on our path. We can start the journey over again by returning to The Dreamer card, or we can try something completely different. The choice is ours.

Symbolism

Archangel Michael stands inside a laurel, which is a symbol of success.

He holds two wands, one for the conscious and the other for the unconscious. We have attained the perfect balance!

In the laurel are the four elements of Fire, Water, Earth, and Air, indicating that we've mastered the use of these elements in creating a beautiful life.

Around the laurel are the landscapes from the four suits of the Minor Arcana, which follow The World card.

Above Michael's head and at his feet is the infinity sign, representing eternal life. We may have accomplished our task, but there will always be far more for us to create!

Angel Number

The number 21 is one of success and creativity. The angels revel in the path that you've followed to this point, and you may even feel an energetic pat on the back. Now you're asked to remain on the path of optimism and positive thinking so that you can attain even more.

Archangel

Archangel Michael, protector of planet Earth, returns for his third and final time, exuding pride in our journey. His colors of royal blue and gold make us feel regal, and his arms open wide in acknowledgment of our accomplishments.

Astrology

Saturn is the planet of testing and challenge. It's said to be the planet where we work through our karma so that we can evolve in this lifetime. Saturn points out where we're restricted or held back. Its association with The World card shows us that we've broken through our barriers. We've been tested and have successfully graduated with full honors!

PART IV

DAY-TO-DAY LIFE
in the
MINOR ARCANA

THE SUIT OF FIRE

Ace of Fire

The Ace of Fire is the first card in a suit that promises many wonderful things. When we draw this card, we have amazing opportunities to change our lives. Aces represent a beginning within the element of their suit. In this case, that is Fire, indicating that new opportunities exist in the areas of creativity, career, passion, and self-development.

Now, we can see that our dreams are within reach; however, we will have to take the actions necessary to attain our goals. This card tells us that wonderful new possibilities are coming into play.

Symbolism

Genies are magical beings who wish to make our dreams come true. This genie has no ulterior motives; he merely wishes to serve. His only reward is to see our happiness fulfilled.

It's said that in order to have a genie appear, it's necessary to rub a magic lamp. The lamp at the bottom of the card tells us that we can make wishes, but it's also necessary to be "hands-on" when the magic starts to happen.

The flowering bush surrounding our genie is called *potentilla* (often referred to as "cinquefoil"). The name *potentilla* comes from the Latin word *potens,* which means to be "powerful, strong, and capable of success."

The five points of the potentilla are said to represent the five senses, and the flowers were worn by medieval knights who'd been successful in their personal quests.

The genie stands between two cities, indicating that there are multiple opportunities for our plans to successfully play out.

In the sky float three moons, mirroring the traditional three wishes said to be offered by genies.

Astrologically, the Moon refers to our emotions, needs, and intuition. All of these are excellent guides in knowing just which wish to make!

Angel Number

This is Card 23. When a magical card like the Ace of Fire shows up, it's very important to keep our thoughts positive. We're in "manifesting mode" with this card, and our beliefs determine what we create. Because of the 3 energy in this number, we may feel inclined to ask for help from ascended masters such as Jesus, the saints, or other spiritual leaders in Heaven. Their assistance dissipates negative energy and keeps our intentions crystal clear.

The number 23 also reduces down to a 5 (2 + 3). Fives are indicators of big changes that are coming into our lives, as well as our power to make modifications to our personal paths, as we're inclined to do.

Astrology

The Aces don't have a specific astrological assessment, but are connected to the element their suit represents—in this case, the suit of Fire. However, the card is attached to the three signs of the zodiac from the element of Fire: Aries, Leo, and Sagittarius.

～

Two of Fire

You've come into your own. New partnerships or contracts. Continue to move forward.

Two of Fire

With the previous card, we were offered wonderful new opportunities. The Two of Fire indicates that we've taken action on the assistance that we were provided, and now the ball is rolling. Still, we're far from finished with our quest; in fact, we've really just begun. It may be time to make a new partnership with someone who can help us move our goals further along. New choices may be required of us, so we should think carefully or ask for the advice of those we trust. Our potential is unlimited!

Symbolism

The two men walking through the forest do so as partners on a quest. They're different from one another, and their strength is enhanced by the diversity of experiences that they bring to the task.

The men are accompanied by a baby dragon who represents the newness of the passion and the fire of their creative endeavor. The dragon is happy and eager to contribute to the adventure in any way he can.

Speckled dragon eggs lie before this trio, indicating that there are still more opportunities available to them. The success they enjoy related to their original purpose may very well give birth to ideas that they're not even aware of yet.

The yellow potentilla flowers from the Ace card (see the Ace of Fire) continue to bloom, proving that success is still ahead of our travelers.

In some cases, this card can indicate gay male relationships when a question relates to that type of romantic partnership. It may also indicate a new relationship that's coming into someone's life, or a current relationship that's being referenced.

Angel Number

This is Card 24. When the Two of Fire shows up, it's likely that we'll be creating some wonderful new partnerships. In this case, some of our new helpers will be angelic in nature, so it's very important to keep our thoughts positive. We're in "manifesting mode" with this card, and our beliefs determine what we create. Heaven sends all the angels we need to dissipate negative energy and keep our intentions crystal clear.

Since the number 24 reduces to 6 (2 + 4), there may be some concerns at this point regarding financial issues. We mustn't let our thoughts focus on worries regarding material concerns, but rather, stay in the joy of what we're creating—with the confidence that the angels will provide us with what we need.

Astrology

This card is associated with Mars in Aries, a very powerful energy for getting things done. It might be a little impulsive, but it has endless exuberance and enthusiasm for the task at hand. New ideas are considered exciting, and change—invigorating!

The energy of Mars in Aries is one of moving quickly and accomplishing great things. Aries is the natural sign for the planet of Mars, so the desire to create and be successful is multiplied. One thing to be aware of with this energy is that partnerships that form may be between two people who have very strong opinions about how things should be done. If compromise and good-natured debate can be maintained, there's very little that can't be accomplished. However, if a stalemate sets in, progress may be slowed.

∼

Abundance! Things look very good; have patience at this time. Make long-term plans.

Three of Fire

It's time to pause and reflect. Certainly, our successes to date have been very encouraging and uplifting. Not all the rewards for our efforts have yet presented themselves, but we know that very soon our "ship will come in." There's no need to wait for its arrival, so why not begin planning for the next phase? What will we create next? How will we expand upon our previous successes? It's time to cast our gaze far out onto the horizon and dream even bigger dreams!

Symbolism

A little girl sits pondering the power of creation that is before her.

Her friend is a young dragon who's been there while all her dreams have come to fruition. Some think her dragon friend is imaginary, but she knows that he's real, just as certainly as she knows that her hopes for the future are real. Or is it possible that the dragon is real and the girl is imaginary? Either way, purity of intention mixed with fiery passion is a recipe for success!

A volcano erupts in the distance, sending out Fire and all the materials necessary to build anything the little girl wants to try her hand at.

While the turbulence of sheer creation rolls in front of her, the little girl and her friend sit in perfect peace, surrounded by a forest that once was as raw and untamed as the landscape in the distance.

Daisies grow to reflect the removal of stress and drama in this moment of the girl's life. She's worked hard, but now she can relax a bit and see to her own care.

In her efforts to create, life has been complicated for the girl, and it will most likely become complicated again when she begins her next project. But for now, what could be simpler than to sit among the daisies with one's best dragon friend?

Angel Number

The Three of Fire is Card 25. The 5 energy beckons the change that's coming for the little girl and her dragon. New plans are being formulated, and while they enjoy where they are right now, they know that there's so much more to come—wonderful things that can only be enjoyed if they soldier on and continue to create. The 2 energy of the number bodes well for their optimism and the positive thoughts they're committing their future to.

This number reduces to 7 (2 + 5), a beautiful number, assuring us that we're on the right path. This number speaks of spiritual growth and magical blessings from Heaven—rewards for our hard work.

Astrology

Astrologically, this card relates to the Sun in Aries. Aries is the first sign in the zodiac, and the Sun is where our astrological charts all begin. So the energy of this combination perfectly matches this card, since it's the very first moment before our work begins.

Aries is a sign of leaders who are fascinated by the quest and personally associate themselves with the results of their efforts. Therefore, the Sun in Aries usually comes from a place of integrity. Dealing with any given situation in an underhanded way just isn't its style.

Aries is a sign that loves a new challenge, so long as it can identify with the goals and see something noble in the pursuit.

~

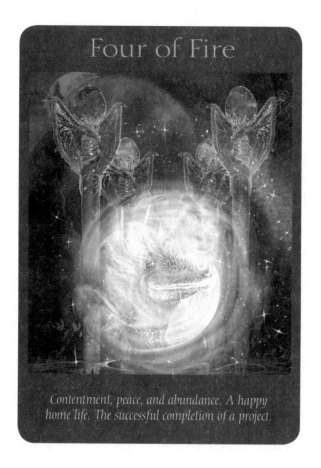

Four of Fire

Contentment, peace, and abundance. A happy home life. The successful completion of a project.

Four of Fire

This is such a wonderful time! Our work has been rewarded; and we feel the comfort of abundance, peace, and the promise of a joyful life. The fruits of our labors have been widely acknowledged as deserved, and our efforts have been appreciated. Financially, we feel a sense of stability. It may even be time to focus on the joys of our home lives. Perhaps we'll get married, start a family, or build a home. Perhaps we'll do all three! It's time to express our gratitude to the wonderful people in our lives . . . as well as to our angels and the Universe.

Symbolism

Four wands stand, forming a square, which is the symbol of structure and balance. The shape provides a sense of stability and safety, much like the life that the Four of Fire presents to us. A square also represents matter, and the things in life we create, such as home and hearth.

The four wands are the colors of the lower four chakras: red, orange, yellow, and green. The Four of Fire isn't a card that's concerned with our spiritual development, but lends itself to feeling safe with a roof over our heads, marriage and procreation, feeling in charge of our lives, and the joy of being in love.

An orb spins between the four wands in a clockwise direction, assuring us that our lives are moving in a positive direction.

A friendly dragon materializes inside the orb to show that our passions and creativity have been brought successfully to life.

When we wish upon a star, it's said that our dreams come true. This card is full of stars to wish upon, indicating that we have faith that many more of our hopes will be brought to fruition.

Angel Number

This is Card 26, blending the power of positive thought with the desire to be financially secure. The Four of Fire is a card that indicates we feel extremely happy (even celebratory!) about our situation at work and at home.

The number 26 reduces to 8 (2 + 6), promising us further prosperity and abundance going forward. Ours is not a temporary situation, but one that indicates continued promise in the foreseeable future for ourselves, our partners, and our children.

Astrology

Astrologically, this card is attributed to Venus in Aries. Venus is a planet of beauty, romance, and creativity—the perfect planet to link to a card that shows us being happy and content with all these aspects of our lives.

Of course, Aries energy makes the desire to achieve our goals quite pressing. We want the lovely things the Four of Fire offers, and we want them *now!* It's that kind of drive that has brought us from the beginning inspiration of the Ace of Fire, through the creation of the Two of Fire, into the long-term planning of the Three of Fire, and into the celebratory joy of the Four of Fire.

~

Five of Fire

It's a fact that sometimes there's conflict in our lives. The conflict may be with others, or with trying to choose which issue requires our attention first. While these challenges may seem to be coming from outside ourselves, the Law of Attraction can sometimes bring people into our lives who can mirror unresolved issues that we've internalized. For this reason, when this card is drawn, it's a good idea to review the possibility that the real difficulty we're facing comes from within.

This card can also represent more benign challenges, such as athletic competitions, contests at work, or other chances to prove ourselves to our peers.

Symbolism

Wands posted into the ground present themselves in a configuration that appears to block our way. We can't get past them or even see what's going on behind them.

Five is the number of change. Without a change in our perception of the situation, or the way in which we're going about our tasks, the barrier will remain.

The flowers that bloomed in the early cards of the suit to indicate great opportunities are now missing (see the Ace of Fire). We need to review the experiences that we're creating for ourselves to validate that they're what we want.

The top three wands appear to dominate the lower two. The upper wands are the colors of the orange sacral chakra (issues regarding our self-worth), the red root chakra (concerns about our basic needs), and the light blue throat chakra (how we communicate). Is it possible that we feel unsafe and are voicing our frustration from these three areas instead of coming from the green heart chakra (emotions such as love), or our violet crown chakra (our spiritual selves)?

Angel Number

This is Card 27. The 2 energy of this number reminds us that if we focus on the positive, then the Law of Attraction will bring it to us. However, if our minds are buried in fear and worry, then anything we're concerned about will come to us. In every challenge there's a lesson that will put us on the right path that comes with the 7 energy.

Together these numbers reduce to 9 (2 + 7), a number of service to ourselves and others, as well as one that brings more light into the world while we're fulfilling our purpose for being on Earth. We need to give thanks for the lessons learned so that our happiness will continue to grow as time goes by.

Astrology

Saturn in Leo is the astrological attribution for the Five of Fire. Saturn is the planet where we feel restricted or limited in what we're trying to accomplish. Leo is known for being a sign that wants to shine and be noticed. It has a strong need to be recognized for its accomplishments and even who or what it is.

The pairing of these two energies can cause us to undervalue ourselves or our goals. Internal conflicts may develop that cause us to stop trying. Then, Heaven, which wants us to be all that we can be, presents us with an external challenge that reflects our inner one. We must break through the five wands that block our progress.

~

Six of Fire

Victory! Good news is on its way.
Public recognition or awards.

Six of Fire

The Six of Fire is one of the cards in tarot that has a nickname: it's the "victory card"! We've made great strides in our journey when this card is drawn. The trouble from the Five of Fire has been resolved, and we've ridden into town to great applause and celebration. Information is headed our way that will make us extremely happy. We may win an award, get a promotion, or perhaps that book contract we've been hoping for will finally make its way to our door.

This card could also mean that we will be recognized for our accomplishments in a very public way. It may be time to do some self-promotion or marketing with the media.

Symbolism

A victorious man arrives into town to great fanfare! His quest has been very successful.

Red rose petals are tossed into the air to lead his way into the village. These flowers are signs of passion and love. Our hero followed his passion, and he receives great admiration from the villagers due to the example he's set.

White horses are generally associated with heroes who display a purity of intention; they imply victory or an impending success. There's also a connection to spiritual development and our intuitive abilities.

Banners bearing the symbol of this suit's icon, a dragon, fly in the background. Flags with dragons on them are associated with King Arthur and his honorable reign, which brought peace and prosperity to Camelot.

The two women in the image are meant to bring a little feminine energy into the card for balance.

Angel Number

This is Card 28. The energy of this number is extremely positive and successful, to match the card. The 2 influence provides the positive thoughts that manifest into joy for the person who drew the card. This same energy has brought in the effects of the 8, to bring prosperity and abundance for our knight's reward.

The number 28 reduces to a 1 (2 + 8 = 10, 1 + 0 = 1). The number 1 not only represents manifesting our desires, but also new beginnings. Now that the knight has attained his desires, he can turn his attention to his next big success!

Astrology

Jupiter in Leo is a very generous energy. Its good fortune is generated by being of service to others and providing an excellent role model. It provides inspiration to others in a win-win, give-and-take way since this energy loves to be in the spotlight. Jupiter in Leo is extremely confident and courageous due to its belief that others can learn and benefit from its experience in overcoming challenges.

~

Seven of Fire

This is a card of feminine power. While the card does ask us to stand our ground and defend what we believe in, it also requests that we ponder our choices. Is this battle worth the fight? Would we be better off letting go of our need to chase after this particular issue, and instead, redirect our focus to something we consider more important? It's certain that we'll grow stronger from the challenge that's before us as long as we make our choices from the heart rather than from the intellect.

Symbolism

A beautiful and confident woman works in concert with her dragon friend.

The dragon appears to be feminine in gender due to the pinks and purples in her coloring.

This reminds us of the Three of Fire card, but here, the young girl has grown up. Instead of contemplating the future, as in the Three of Fire card, the young woman and the dragon team up to defend their beliefs and create the future they've planned.

The young woman carries a wand that is the color of the heart chakra, showing us that her actions relate to love, and are worth defending.

Six wands fly toward our heroine. Six is the angel number of material concerns; however, since she's carrying the wand of the heart, she's sure to prevail.

Angel Number

This is Card 29, a number that calls for us to be strong and focused on our life purpose. This number, the card, and the astrology (see the next section) are extremely certain of themselves. Confidence is the determining factor in success; in fact, the definition of success is ours to determine.

The number 29 reduces to 11. Unlike most numbers, 11 is a master number and therefore does not get further reduced. This is a very powerful number that assures our ability to manifest. The young woman on the dragon is sure to succeed in her quest!

Astrology

Mars in Leo is very passionate and confident in its actions. It has a powerful need to be relevant in the world and to make a difference. Often it can be fearless in its ambitions and will take actions that are strong and sometimes overwhelming. We may not agree with the quest that Mars in Leo has undertaken, but there's no doubt that it will follow its heart to the ends of the earth!

~

Eight of Fire

Events moving at a fast pace. Delays are over. Many things happening at once.

Eight of Fire

This card can be summed up in three words: *busy, busy, busy!* When the Eight of Fire card is drawn, it often reflects someone who's filled to the brim with things to do. It can also indicate a person for whom things have been very quiet but who's about to see an end to the slow times. This is a card of rapid shifts and activity. Because of the astrology of this card, it's most often a very welcome change. We may feel a bit harried about all that we have to do, but we're happy to have so much activity in our lives. We may feel stressed, but it's stress that comes from positive things.

Symbolism

Eight wands fly off into the sky, giving the impression of fireworks. Fireworks are a sign of great celebration! If we're lucky, they're beautifully orchestrated. However, sometimes fireworks are unpredictable and a little chaotic.

The wands don't appear to all be headed in the same direction. Clearly, there are multiple, and perhaps even competing, goals to be accomplished. It may be necessary to prioritize our efforts.

While this is a Fire card, in the background we see a body of water. It would be easy to let our emotions carry us away, but our purposes are served by keeping our feelings grounded and on an even keel.

Angel Number

The Eight of Fire is Card 30. This number assures us that we're loved and supported by Source and the ascended masters as we take charge of this exciting time in our lives. We can think of the fireworks imagery in the card as a celebration in Heaven, cheering us on as we follow our life path!

This card reduces to 3 (3 + 0), further emphasizing the message of celebration!

Astrology

Mercury in Sagittarius is an extremely optimistic energy. Since Mercury rules the mind, this astrological association indicates that our minds are so full of wonderful ideas that we don't even know where to start. Our perception of the future is very bright even if our to-do list is brimming over. We may feel restless, and eager to get going. We'd probably love to roll up our sleeves and do everything ourselves, as we're very independent—but the truth is that we'll probably need a little help from friends, peers, or people who work for us.

～

Don't give up. Protect that which you've created. Have courage, and believe in yourself.

Nine of Fire

The Nine of Fire indicates that we feel the need to protect what we've created. All through our journey in the Fire suit, we've worked hard to create our dreams. We may feel uncomfortable about the safety or stability of what we've built and feel the need to redouble our efforts. It's important at this moment that we have absolute confidence in ourselves. We need to go within to access our inner courage and then turn it outward in a show of bravery and determination. As long as we believe in ourselves, all will be well!

Symbolism

A beautiful woman stands ready, determined, and perhaps even a bit defiant. She's proud of her accomplishments and will never give up on her dreams.

Beside her is her dragon ally, who has her wings up as if to protect what's behind her.

The dragon and the woman both hold wands that are the same color, indicating that they're invested as equal partners in what has been created.

A pot of gold represents what has been accomplished. This may be taken literally as financial abundance, or as a metaphor that the results of their passion are as valuable to them as gold.

In the pot of gold there are six additional wands. This may indicate that their worries over their possessions is unwarranted, since the number 6 can indicate undue concern about **material goods**.

Angel Number

This is Card 31. We're asked to assess whether our fears or worries may simply be illusions. Perhaps our protective stance isn't necessary; however, if our concerns are justified, then we can know with great confidence that our determination will see us through. Help from the ascended masters is ours for the asking.

Since this number reduces to 4 (3 + 1), we can also know that the entire angelic realm is by our side!

Astrology

The astrological association for this card is Moon in Sagittarius. This is a very independent and confident energy. While it can sometimes be competitive, it also stands for a sense of safety and protection. There's a belief that everything will work out even in the face of extreme odds. Visionary, hopeful, and perhaps even a bit sassy, Moon in Sagittarius can accomplish just about anything it wants!

~

Too much work. Accept help from others. Life is out of balance. Stress-related health concerns.

Ten of Fire

Work can be fulfilling and exciting, or it can be exhausting and feel like a chore. This card represents times in our lives when we're working entirely too much without leaving any space for fun and play. Often this card shows up when people are working multiple jobs, or when single parents are dealing with the challenge of working all day and then caring for their kids when they get home. We may find ourselves so intensely involved in our current endeavors that we don't even realize how rundown we're becoming.

This card can also indicate health problems that are created by overwork. We can take the Ten of Fire as a possible message to reduce our workload, take time off, or delegate tasks to others when possible.

Symbolism

The dragon carries a heavy burden, and does so alone. The woman from the Nine of Fire card is no longer there to assist.

The pot of gold from the Nine of Fire is still intact, but now there are ten wands in it, not only making it heavier, but giving it a more intense energy.

The dragon flies at night over a starlit city. Perhaps the dragon has been working into the night, or maybe this is a second job or after-hours project.

Since dragons represent passion in the *Angel Tarot Cards,* the dragon's stance indicates that passion has been worn down by overwork.

Angel Number

This card's angel number is 32, which asks us to have faith—to believe that our circumstances are in our best interests, and that any struggle we may be feeling is temporary, and will give way to the joy of knowing that we're on a path that will make us happier over time. It's a good idea for us to work with the ascended masters (especially Jesus, in this case) to ask that our burdens be lightened and our challenges simply fade away.

This number reduces to 5 (3 + 2), a number of great change. In order to extricate ourselves from this time of weariness, the changes our angels are asking us to make must be implemented.

Astrology

Saturn is the planet that represents where we feel restricted or held back. Sagittarius, on the other hand, is a planet of great freedom and independence. So it's no surprise that these two are very challenging when in combination. Saturn binds Sagittarius's natural spiritual faith, making it difficult to have hope. It's tough to cope if we don't have faith. Saturn in Sagittarius can become very disillusioned, frustrated, and skeptical. This energy believes that we only attain success through hard work, and trust must be earned.

~

Page of Fire

The Page of Fire is a very exciting card to choose! New opportunities present themselves to us, and we may get some information about something wonderful that's coming into our lives. This is a highly creative card where our ability to "think outside the box" is extremely valuable. We're asked to follow our passions and to let them guide us to our lifework. Without question, we're asked to use our own unique brand of magic to manifest our happiness. This card can also mean a promotion, career change, or any new and promising development in our professional lives.

Symbolism

A beautiful young woman is in the process of manifesting what she desires. We can call it magic, or we can call it the passion of following our dreams. Either way, it's her belief in herself that paves the way to fulfillment.

The young woman's friend is a magical dragon with gemstones in its wings. Gemstones are precious and glitter with many colors of light, much like the unique and invaluable dream of every individual.

A phoenix is a bird that is said to be reborn from its own ashes. The girl on the card is bringing forth just such a bird to show her intention to re-create her life.

A beautiful white city shines behind the girl and the dragon. White is the color of purity of intention, and a city represents humankind's ability to manifest. It also reflects a possible home full of like-minded people for our young lady and her dragon friend.

Angel Number

This is Card 33, a very powerful number that reflects a direct connection to ascended masters and spiritual leaders. In fact, 33 is a master number, which means that it doesn't reduce down to 6, but remains 33. This master number is for those who want to serve humankind by doing good works in the world. The number is one of a teacher and leader who can help others see their purpose and inspire them to focus on others rather than themselves.

People

The Page of Fire is very exciting to be around—filled with incredible exuberance and enthusiasm for whatever is about to be undertaken. The Page is willing to assume the lead on any creative project, and there is nothing new she isn't willing to try. The Page's inherent joy makes her fun to be around, and her happiness is contagious.

Of course, that kind of dynamic energy can be a little hard to manage. Before we can give a Page of Fire instructions, she's probably already run off and completed half of the project. It may also be difficult for her to keep her focus on one thing for very long.

Astrology

The Pages in tarot don't represent a particular astrological attribution, but are associated with a season and a geographical area of the world. The Page of Fire represents spring and the continent of Asia.

~

Knight of Fire

There are times in our lives when situations we hadn't anticipated require us to move quickly. It doesn't have to be a challenge that worries us; it might simply be something wonderful to consider—like having multiple job offers but a short period of time to decide. We wouldn't want to make a rash decision, but we're probably going to have to come to a conclusion pretty quickly. Thinking is important, but our feelings will probably tell us more about what we want to do. We need to consider all our options in great detail, and then off we'll go!

Symbolism

A handsome Knight gallops into our field of view. It's easy to imagine him asking, "How may I help you?"

His white horse tells us that we can expect to be very successful in our endeavor. Our intentions are honorable, and we need have nothing to fear.

Our Knight carries with him a wand rather than a sword. The solution to our challenges comes from passion and creativity rather than intellect.

Behind the Knight is a body of water, indicating that he's riding along the shoreline. The elements of Water, Earth (the shore), and Fire (his wand) tell us that we will trust our feelings and passions in a balanced way in order to make our choice.

Angel Number

The number for our Knight is 34, which indicates that we need not worry—we have a great deal of help from our angels and the ascended masters. In much the same way that this Knight in shining armor shows up to assist us, so too do our protectors in Heaven. This number reduces to 7 (3 + 4) to show us that we're on the right path and need not be preoccupied with the results!

People

Sometimes unexpected things just come up, but the Knight of Fire is here to save the day! And save us he most certainly will do, since that's the type of quest he lives for. This Knight has it all under control—clearly able to accomplish ten things at once. He moves very quickly, all the while flashing us a charming smile. He loves adventure and is confident in his ability to succeed.

Just keep him busy, because this Knight gets restless very easily. If there's no damsel in distress, no day to save, or no world to keep protected from injustice, then he's likely to wander off to other parts of the world where his considerable skills are needed.

Astrology

The Knight is Leo, with a bit of Cancer thrown in. He loves the spotlight that his adventures bring him, but he also cares about those he's "rescuing." Both Leo and Cancer have a penchant for the dramatic, so expect our Knight to be bigger than life. Still, beneath that fiery exterior, which is seemingly made up of only passion and flash, resides a heart as good as gold.

~

Queen of Fire

What are we waiting for? There's nothing we can't accomplish! This is a card of incredible creativity and passion just waiting to be ignited. The Queen of Fire wants us to understand our unlimited inner strength and inexhaustible power. We mustn't be afraid to present ourselves to the world with beauty and grace. This card also indicates the ability to balance many aspects of life—especially career and family issues.

Symbolism

A beautiful, fiery Queen sits upon a throne of emeralds, which are the jewels of the heart. It indicates an open heart chakra, as well as the ability to awaken the spirituality of ourselves and others.

A bracelet adorns the Queen's wrist, and it is also made of emeralds. Our ability to glide through any situation is assured as long as our movements are determined by our hearts.

The Queen has a wand of fire from which she creates, and she only chooses endeavors that she's very passionate about.

The Queen's fire is giving birth to a bejeweled dragon. It's not necessary for her to create on her own when she can do so with a friend. This card indicates that friends and helpers will be easy to come by.

The Queen wears angel wings, the only card in this suit to do so. She loves to help others and will extend aid whenever possible.

Angel Number

The Queen of Fire is Card 35. With the 5 energy in this number, we're reminded that we're all manifesters of our realities. We can make the changes we wish in our lives at any time. We also have the help of the ascended masters and all their combined experience.

The number 35 reduces to 8 (3 + 5). With the 8 energy in this number, we're reminded that this card is one of manifestation and creation. Abundance and prosperity are available to all those who draw this card!

People

The Queen of Fire can handle more things at once than probably any other court card in the deck! She's a masterful multitasker who's also so charming that she usually has friends swarming all around her. Her family adores her because they are her first priority. However, this doesn't keep her from rising through the ranks to become president of a company, a famous author, or the owner of a successful business.

She's very independent, and her brilliance usually allows her to have her own way. Should you choose to go into business with this Queen, you'll want to make sure your visions match hers. If you're on the same wavelength as she is, you'll be able to write a beautiful story, but if you have ideas contrary to hers that you feel strongly about, you might want to choose a different partner.

Astrology

The Queen of Fire is Aries, with a generous helping of Pisces. Aries is the sign of getting amazing things done. It's the beginning of the zodiac and is therefore focused on creating. Pisces is a very caring and intuitive sign that senses the needs of others. It's easy to see how these two signs combine to create such a passionate and nurturing person.

~

King of Fire

It's time to take charge! This card wants us to realize that we have incredible leadership skills. There are many who would benefit from our vision and ability to focus and get the job done effectively and efficiently, but also with a bit of flair. It's time to really focus on the issues that matter, and dismiss those that are just distractions. Talented and friendly people can also show up to help, so we need to graciously accept their assistance!

Symbolism

Our King wears a headdress of peacock feathers—symbols of royalty, integrity, and immortality. Peacock feathers are also associated with Quan-Yin, who's known for her loving-kindness and her desire to help others.

The dragon that we've watched grow up throughout this suit is now fully grown and represents a powerful ally and friend to our King.

The dragon's feathers have matured to be mostly purple and violet, which is associated with the crown chakra. There is a oneness with Spirit and the ability to provide the wisdom necessary to solve any situation.

Angel Number

The angel number for this card is 36, which asks us to keep our thoughts away from fear when it comes to material things, and to stay focused on what matters in life. The number is also associated with ascended masters such as Quan-Yin and Jesus, who are kind and loving and only harbor the best of intentions for us.

The number 36 reduces to 9 (3 + 6), a number that asks us to be of service to others and to seek out our life purpose and begin fulfilling it immediately.

People

This King is charismatic and charming, an inspiring speaker who's able to motivate people to do amazing things. He's almost certainly a leader in his chosen field, or even the community at large. He's also an amazing father (which makes him the perfect mate for the Queen of Fire), and he truly loves his family. Still, he does crave attention, so things will go more smoothly if we give it to him. If we try to upstage him, he'll leave us standing there alone.

Astrology

This King is mostly Sagittarius, but with a splash of Scorpio. Sagittarius is an optimistic, happy sign that loves to teach, learn new things, and travel. Scorpio is more inwardly focused and tends to want to understand its inner world. Together, they create energy that is very enlightened about what it is while also reaching out to the world with a positive outlook.

∼

THE SUIT OF WATER

Ace of Water

Falling in love or the resurgence of a relationship.
Spiritual growth and enhanced intuition. A new home.

Ace of Water

The Ace of Water is a wonderful card that indicates heart-warming emotions and honest connections with others. Usually it heralds a beautiful new romance, but it can signify a very close and intimate (but platonic) friendship as well. This card also represents a time of deepening spiritual and psychic experiences.

The Aces always speak of something new within their suit. In this case, that would be beginnings that relate to emotions, family, and intuition. This card can also refer to a new home.

Symbolism

A handsome young merman swims down to reach for a cup. It's just slightly beyond his reach, but soon the cup will be his.

A cup is a vessel for water, the element for this suit as well as the universal sign for emotions.

The tip of the merman's tail is just over the top of the waterline. He's almost completely committed to the emotional experience that will soon present itself, but there's a small part of him that's unsure.

The water is a bit turbulent above, but near the bottom, all is peaceful. This emotional experience will quiet our fears and bring us comfort.

Angel Number

The Ace of Water is Card 37. This is a beautiful energy meant to assure us that we're following our true and perfect path. Heavenly magic is at work, opening doors for us in all our relationships. All we need do is forge ahead and walk through!

The number reduces to a 1 (3 + 7 = 10, 1 + 0 = 1), a number that tells us that our thoughts are directing what we create, so we need to focus on the future we desire.

Astrology

Aces have no specific astrological assessment, but are connected instead to the element their suit represents—in this case, Water. They also represent the three signs of the zodiac that reflect this element: Cancer, Scorpio, and Pisces.

~

A relationship that continues to grow closer.
Forgiveness. The positive resolution of a conflict.

Two of Water

This is the card of falling in love. In the Ace of Water, we meet someone, but the Two of Water shows that the relationship has grown. Hearts have become intertwined, and the commitments between those involved have grown deeper. This card can also represent very close friends who've made a connection that will last their entire lives.

This is also a card of forgiveness. Disputes between lovers or friends fade away. If we're involved in a relationship, either romantic or platonic, that has been strained or troubled, we have to remember not to give up. The situation can be resolved in a positive and mutually beneficial way.

Symbolism

A mermaid and merman have come together at the bottom of the ocean. They're not afraid to explore the depths of their emotions together.

Dolphins swim around the couple, representing playfulness, community, and harmony—qualities that any relationship benefits from.

The mermaid and merman have placed their cups together to show their desire to have their emotional worlds support one another. However, they haven't poured their two cups *together,* signifying the importance of maintaining their individuality.

There are yellow angelfish swimming around to let us know that these two merpeople are very much emotionally connected. These fish also represent spiritual growth and evolution. And of course, angels are watching over this relationship.

The "flame angelfish" in the card show us the passion the two merpeople feel for one another—the flame of love is very much alive.

Angel Number

Deep emotional involvements create big changes in our lives. This card's number is 38. With the 8 energy in this number, we're reminded that this card is one of manifestation and creation. An abundance of love is available to those who draw the Two of Water!

The number 38 reduces to 11 (3 + 8), but doesn't reduce further since 11 is a master number. This is a perfect number for a relationship inspired by the Two of Water; we can explore the unlimited depths of our emotional and spiritual worlds.

Astrology

Venus in Cancer is a very loving and nurturing energy. It desires and attracts deep romantic relationships and may feel somewhat out of sorts unless such a partnership exists. Words are secondary to feelings or actions with this combination. Venus in Cancer wants to care for others and provide emotional support; however, it also wants to feel that same tenderness and connection returned in equal measure.

∼

Three of Water

Now we get to celebrate! This card is famous for pointing out a reason to proclaim our happiness over a joyous event. Often, this card heralds the announcement of an engagement, a wedding, the birth of a child, a graduation, or the promotion of someone to a new job.

Or perhaps we don't need a reason to kick up our heels. This card may be telling us that we need to enjoy life a little more and find a reason to have a party. We might enchant our inner child with a day at an amusement park—or whatever makes our hearts sing—and embrace the moment and have fun!

Symbolism

Three happy dolphins swim about in the ocean. Dolphins have very strong connections to those in their groups. For this reason, they represent happy communities.

Three cups full of water sit together on the ocean's floor. These cups represent the contents of our emotional, inner lives. By placing the cups together, the dolphins have shown their desire to have a shared experience.

A ray of light softly shines through the water to the dolphins and the cups. At that level of the ocean, we would expect the image to be dark, but these happy circumstances have invited us into the light.

Angel Number

The angel number for this card is 39, which asks us to be of service to others, seek out our life purpose, and begin fulfilling it immediately so that we may have the joy of celebration in our lives every day. The number is also associated with ascended masters such as Quan-Yin and Jesus, who are kind and loving and have only our best interests at heart.

The number 39 reduces to 3 (3 + 9 = 12, 1 + 2 = 3). In traditional numerology, this is a number of creativity, communication, and artfulness, which are all aspects of the Three of Water.

Astrology

Mercury in Cancer is an energy that tends to communicate with great feeling. Even though Mercury is most often thought of as the mental aspect in astrology, the deeply feeling Cancer softens the temptation to intellectualize everything when it might be best to feel its way through things. This aspect is concerned with family lineage and heritage, and anything that may have happened in the past. For this reason, events such as weddings, births, and graduations become all the more important.

~

Four of Water

Missing an opportunity. Discontentment or boredom. Open your eyes to the possibilities.

Four of Water

The Four of Water is a friendly reminder from Heaven that we may be missing an important message. Sometimes when we're very focused on the day-to-day, we don't notice that others (or our angels) are offering us a lovely opportunity. We need to stand back from the situation, look around, and ask ourselves or our angels, "What beautiful possibility might be around the next corner?"

We may be aware of something good that came our way, but perhaps we dismissed it as not being of value or not what we wanted at the time. The Four of Water would ask us to reconsider. Perhaps the option we said *no* to is better than we think. Or maybe taking full advantage of the opportunity will lead us to what we want.

Symbolism

A mermaid is so focused on the three cups in front of her that she doesn't notice anything else that's going on around her.

The three cups that have caught her attention are in the back of the image (the past), and are also in the dark (no longer lighting up her life).

A single cup sits in the light—a golden-rimmed opportunity just waiting for the mermaid to see and realize its potential.

Angel Number

The number for the Four of Water is 40. Those who draw this card may find themselves feeling as if their situations are complex and difficult to solve; however, this beautiful number assures them that they have the help of the Divine and the angels at their side. There's nothing that the angels can't help them work through.

The number reduces to 4 (4 + 0), further emphasizing the presence of angels at this time.

Astrology

The energy of Moon in Cancer carries with it a striking depth of emotion and intimacy. However, it can also become distracted by what's going on around it. It can become somewhat self-absorbed and focused on the past (like the three cups in the back of the image). Due to this aspect's deep concern for family and home, it may also not notice gifts from Heaven that are offered to it because it's so busy taking care of others.

$\sim$

Five of Water

Things not turning out the way you'd hoped. Not seeing the positive in a situation. Crying over spilled milk.

Five of Water

We can't always see what would be best for us. It is therefore natural that things don't always turn out in the way we'd envisioned they would. However, the Universe knows what's best for us even if we don't see the path that it has laid out for us. What's important during these times is to refocus our minds and hearts and believe that our situation will serve us in the long run. Focusing on the past or the things that went "wrong" only keeps us from moving forward in the direction of our eventual happiness.

Symbolism

Three broken cups lie in the darkness. It's almost difficult to see them, which prompts the question "Are these even meant to be seen anymore?"

The three broken cups are nearly buried at the bottom of the ocean in the sand. The message here is to "bury the past."

Two of the cups are sitting in the light, upright and ready to be enjoyed. This is where our focus should be.

Bubbles can be seen floating around the cups that are in the light. The bottom of the ocean is a place where we would be challenged to breathe, and yet the bubbles indicate that there's air to be found—telling us that there's hope if we follow the signs.

Angel Number

The Five of Water resonates to the angel number 41, which tells us that our thoughts are creating the reality that we're living. If we want to make new choices, we can create a new life for ourselves that's happy and fulfilling.

This number reduces to 5 (4 + 1), the number of change. Fortunately in the case of the Five of Water, we can choose to change ourselves and seize control over how this change occurs.

Astrology

Mars in Scorpio is one of the most intense aspects. This energy doesn't shy away from exploring any part of life, and therefore it may forget to walk away from past disappointments. Since it isn't afraid to fully immerse itself in what may have once been troubling, it doesn't feel the same impulse to leave it behind that others may feel.

~

Six of Water

*Memories from your history or childhood.
Issues regarding children. Romanticizing the past.*

Six of Water

The past has a significant influence over our present and even the future. The Six of Water card reminds us to honor that past by expressing gratitude for our beautiful memories and to be forgiving regarding challenging times. This card may indicate that someone from our past is going to return to our lives. It may be someone whom we grew up with, or perhaps someone we knew from our early years as an adult. Because of this card's watery energy, this person from our past may be someone we had a romantic history with, or someone who was once a friend but who will become something more intimate in the future. The card can also ask us to review how we see the past. Are we making it more dramatic than it was? More lovely than the reality actually was?

The Six of Water often has to do with children. It's an indicator of pregnancy, a matter involving our current children, or even a sign that the person who drew the card should or does work with children professionally. It can also remind us to *be* like a child, and allow more fun into our lives. The Six of Water can signify receiving or exchanging gifts as well.

Symbolism

Two joyful merchildren play in the ocean. The children represent the past, and the ocean symbolizes emotional memories.

The boy has his head above water, showing that he's seeing things not through the eyes of emotion, but rather through the eyes of intellect. His gaze, however, is turned back to the ocean (his feelings). This reminds us that sometimes we need to objectively observe our memories of the past rather than doing so emotionally.

The girl, in contrast, is completely submerged beneath the ocean. Her body language is one of sheer happiness. She isn't rationalizing *how* the past happened or *why* it happened, but is only reveling in the fact that it has made her who she is.

When this card is drawn, we can get important information about what is happening with our client by noticing whom our eyes are drawn to: the boy or the girl.

Six cups are scattered around the card. They represent memories, especially emotional ones. The cups in the back of the card, or in the dark, symbolize memories that are further back in time and more difficult to remember fully. Other cups are more in the light, signifying more current memories.

Angel Number

The angel number for the Six of Water is 42, which tells us to keep the faith. We can look to our past for guidance regarding the choices we've made that suited us. Or we can use our history to remind us of the mistakes we wish to avoid in the future.

This number reduces to 6 (4 + 2), which is a symbol for material items such as gifts, one of the meanings of this card.

Astrology

Sun in Scorpio is the astrological attribution of this card. Scorpio is a deeply feeling sign that's able to delve far into the ocean of emotion that signifies its inner world. Memories are stored as much in feelings as in thoughts. If Sun in Scorpio feels wronged or betrayed, it can be very difficult to forgive the situation and move forward.

∼

Seven of Water

A complex decision. The need to do research. Stop procrastinating!

Seven of Water

The Seven of Water is a card of indecision and the need to make choices. When we find ourselves unable to choose between various or contradictory options, we can fall into inaction. Our dreams don't move forward, and our lives feel stalled. Sometimes the answer to finding the right action to take lies in doing more research; other times, we're merely procrastinating. This card asks us to do whatever is necessary to move forward.

The Seven of Water card is also a possible indicator of addiction, so if the question we're asking has to do with dependency or unhealthy behaviors, drawing this card would lead us to believe that there's cause for concern.

Symbolism

Seven cups lie at the bottom of the ocean, and each one is filled with a colored light of one of the chakras. The answer to our question lies in which color our eyes are drawn to. From left to right on the image of the card, the colors are:

- **Dark blue:** The third-eye chakra speaks to our intuitive gifts, our integrity, and taking responsibility for our actions.

- **Purple:** The crown chakra relates to concerns or solutions to problems that focus on our spirituality and the way in which we understand ourselves.

- **Green:** The heart chakra is one of love, compassion for others, and listening to our feelings for guidance. It also relates to forgiveness.

- **Red:** The base or root chakra refers to the ways in which we feel safe and provided for; issues such as home, finances, and self-confidence are key.

- **Orange** (the cup at the front of the card): The sacral chakra governs issues related to creativity. This can also include sexuality and reproduction. Dependency issues are also possible.

- **Yellow** (to the right of the red light): The solar-plexus chakra represents where we feel either empowered or without power in our lives.

- **Light blue:** The throat chakra is related to issues of communication (or lack thereof) and the way in which we speak our truths.

Angel Number

This card is number 43. Here, we have the combined power of the angels and ascended masters to help us make the choices we need to make. We have no worries, knowing that with their help, we can't make a poor decision.

This number reduces to 7 (4 + 3). Removing ourselves from procrastination will place us on the right path.

Astrology

Venus in Scorpio offers many beautiful possibilities. It cares that we have what we want, but without action, we can never be certain that what we thought we wanted is the true desire of the heart.

~

Eight of Water

*A desire to move on. The search
for something more meaningful.
Spiritual and emotional growth.*

Eight of Water

There are many cards in tarot that indicate that a change is coming. However, the Eight of Water card indicates that the choice to go in another direction is fully our own. We feel restless, and that which fascinated us in the past no longer entices us. Instead, we yearn for something more meaningful and wish to have a life that rewards us with emotional and spiritual satisfaction.

Of course, even the decisions we make on our own can be challenging or even bring about great sadness, but that doesn't stop us from doing what is necessary in order to be who we know we're meant to be deep down.

Symbolism

A merman has turned his back on the cups in the foreground. They used to mean something to him and at one time brought him joy, but now their allure is gone.

As he swims away, he heads toward the light, which represents the spiritual evolution and awakening that comes with following our destiny.

The majority of the cups are in the dark, showing that they're not the path to happiness for our merman. As he follows the light and gets farther and farther away, all of the cups will be in darkness, and his attachment to them will be broken.

Angel Number

The Eight of Water is Card 44, a magical number that lets us know we're surrounded by angels. The situation we find ourselves in is completely safe as long as we listen to and follow the guidance our angels are providing us.

This number reduces to 8 (4 + 4), telling us that we'll experience an abundance of emotional fulfillment due to the path we're choosing.

Astrology

Saturn in Pisces is a highly sensitive energy and can be very giving to others—almost too much—which can distract it from its own desires. In the end, Saturn in Pisces wants to be able to know that there's something greater than itself (or its current reality) out there waiting. It wants to manifest its dreams as evidence that there's true meaning in life.

$\sim$

Your wish comes true!
Concerns fade away. A love of life.

Nine of Water

Nine of Water is one of those cards in tarot with a nickname: it's the "wish-comes-true card." This is one of the most joyful cards in the deck and lets us know that our dreams are coming to fruition and that we have much to be joyful and grateful about. If this card jumps from the deck while we're shuffling, it's a good time to make a wish.

This card can also indicate enjoying great luxury and the beautiful things in life.

Symbolism

The mermaid in the image is very happy; she's heard that her wishes will be coming true!

The mermaid has her head above water, so she can't see the beautiful things underwater. Even though she hasn't yet witnessed her good fortune, she has faith that it will come to pass.

There are nine cups under the water, filled to the brim with jewels. However, this card doesn't restrict itself to desires for financial abundance. It can represent wishes related to career, love, health, or whatever we're hoping for.

The jewels are also reflective of this card's reference to luxurious material comforts.

In the background, we can see that there's water coming off the mountain to replenish the ocean. This is to remind us that there's no limit to the Universe. Our good fortune doesn't take away from others, and there's no lack. There's always more than enough for everyone.

Angel Number

The Nine of Water resonates to the number 45. *Change* is the key word when 5 energy is at work, and this card always brings about wonderful new developments in our lives. We need to thank our angels for the blessings we're now receiving.

The number 45 reduces to 9 (4 + 5). The experiences that come with this card can help us grow and evolve so that we may be prepared to follow our life path.

Astrology

Jupiter in Pisces rules the Nine of Water card. Jupiter is the planet of expansiveness and good fortune. Pisces is a sign of sensitive, caring, and compassionate people, so the energy of this astrological attribution tells us that the joyful news of our wish coming true is a karmic reward for our kindness to others and to the world.

~

A contented and rewarding family
life. Your emotional and material needs
are met. Trustworthy relationships.

Ten of Water

The Ten of Water is another card of good fortune. It really does represent "having it all." We've found great contentment in our lives: our relationships are positive and affirming, and we have healthy and strong connections with our children. There's harmony with our friends and extended family, our emotional needs are fulfilled, and we have what we need financially to be happy.

This card can also refer to taking care of family members or allowing others to take care of us.

Symbolism

Many of the elements of the previous cards in the suit of Water have finally come together.

The happy couple from the Two of Water continues to offer their cups (emotional openness) to one another.

The children of the Six of Water indicate that they've now created a very happy family.

The yellow angelfish show that the family is growing and evolving spiritually as a group, with the love and protection of the angels around them.

Angel Number

The angel number for this card is 46. The energy here is one of being aware of our spiritual selves. We can be of service to our families in a selfless manner by teaching them that we're all Divine children of God.

The number 46 reduces to 1 (4 + 6 = 10, 1 + 0 = 1). All relationships will benefit from positive thoughts and a sense of faith. Negativity is likely to bring us challenges that we don't want.

Astrology

Mars in Pisces is a gentle and loving energy. While Mars is usually a very forward-moving planet, when it's in Pisces, it has more of a tendency to just let life happen as it may. It doesn't buck the natural flow of events, but instead feels content to work with things as they are.

~

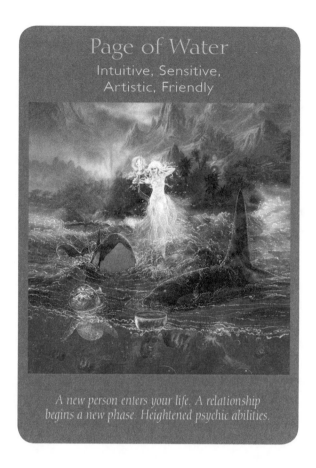

Page of Water

It's always exciting when someone new enters our lives, especially when the nature of the relationship is romantic. It can be just as wonderful when a relationship moves to the next level. An example of that might be when people who've been dating for a while decide to get engaged. These are the types of moments that the Page of Water brings us. Remember that the Pages of tarot are often messengers, so this card can also indicate a love letter or any type of communication of emotion.

The women in the Water suit are very intuitive, so this Page may also indicate new psychic experiences or an increase in our natural gifts.

Symbolism

A beautiful mermaid floats above very tumultuous waters. Since Water represents our feelings, clearly something significant has entered her emotional life.

Our mermaid is surrounded by whales, which symbolize the ability to go within and understand ourselves. They also represent psychic abilities.

The mermaid carries a scepter with a bright light on top of it. This is a beacon to her beloved that she's ready to be found.

Dolphins tell us to have fun! When new emotional experiences come into our lives, it works best if we can keep from being overly serious.

A cup of water floats above the choppy waves. This is to remind us that when our hearts are so completely immersed in a situation, it helps if we keep our heads above water so that we can remain balanced and not get too carried away.

Behind the mermaid is a desertlike landscape. She's come from a place that wasn't fertile with nurturing energy, so she has swum farther out into the waters where there are more opportunities.

Angel Number

The number for the Page of Water card is 47. This is a very evolved energy that walks with the Divine and the angels every day. We can trust the feelings and psychic messages that we receive at this time.

The number 47 reduces to the master number 11 (4 + 7), which does not reduce further. The number 11 tells us that our positive thoughts regarding ourselves and others will manifest in everyone's best interests.

People

The Page of Water is a very kind, sensitive, and dreamy person. If we approach her, we will be welcomed with open arms and a hug so heartfelt that we're likely to be overwhelmed. Of course, we may have to be the one to do the approaching, as our Page is very shy. Love and romance are new to her, so she may be quite timid. Yet she's also a hopeless romantic.

Keep in mind that she experiences the world with her heart. If it's a heart-to-heart conversation we're seeking, she's our gal! If we want to intellectualize our situation, she's likely to just stare back at us blankly with nothing much to say.

Astrology

The Pages in tarot don't represent a particular astrological attribution, but are associated with a season and a geographical area of the world. The Page of Water represents summer and the lands of the Pacific.

~

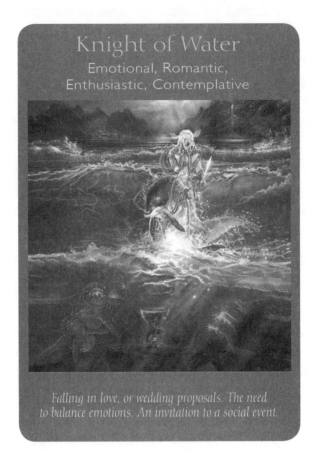

Knight of Water

While the Page of Water heralds our first indicator of a powerful new emotional experience, the Knight of Water shows that
we've been completely swept off our feet! This card refers to falling
in love, offers of marriage, or any romantic experience that causes
us to swoon. In fact, we may be thrown quite off balance by the
entire situation and forget to remain grounded. This card can also
herald an invitation to a social event of some kind.

Symbolism

A handsome merman Knight comes galloping into our lives. He's making some pretty big waves as he arrives.

His companion is a dolphin, indicating that he's here to bring a note of playfulness.

He and the dolphin jump from the water, showing our Knight's ability to move from one emotional situation to another.

The Knight wears a winged helmet, signifying that he can move very quickly into our lives.

Unlike the Page of Water, the image in this card shows the cup completely submerged, indicating that we may very well be "in over our heads."

Angel Number

The Knight of Water is Card 48. We're reminded that our angels are with us and answering our prayers as long as we remember to ask for their assistance. Since 8 is a number of expansion, we can anticipate an abundance of emotion during this time.

The number reduces to 3 (4 + 8 = 12, 1 + 2 = 3). We have the choice to ask the ascended masters for their help as well. The number 3 is also traditionally related to communication, which is very important when dealing with the Knight of Water.

People

The Knight of Water will sweep us completely off our feet! There will be poetry, roses, chocolates, or whatever it is that makes our heart go pitter-patter. This Knight practically invented the concept of romance, and we may never have felt so enamored.

However, we do have to be cautious. The Knight of Water may very well be our one true love, or he may just be a fling. We have to ask the right questions to truly discern if he's in love with us, or just in love with the whole wonderful feeling of *being* in love. It can be difficult to tell. Don't forget that in the image on the card, the Knight is jumping out of one wave into the next one. He can jump from one relationship to another just as easily.

Astrology

Our Knight is Scorpio with a healthy dose of Libra thrown in for good measure. The Scorpio part of his world is extremely deep, emotional, and passionate. However, it's not uncommon that the Libra part could love the "chase" aspect of romance the most. Once the Knight has caught us, he might lose interest.

～

Queen of Water
Tenderhearted, Empathetic,
Patient, Loving

*Relationships develop to a new level. Trust
your intuition. Care for yourself and others.*

Queen of Water

This is a deeply emotional card, asking us to care for others, but to also see that we nurture ourselves just as much. Feelings run deep when this card is drawn, and there's likely to be something very significant going on in our relationships (whether romantic or platonic).

This is also a card of profound psychic experiences. We're asked to listen to our guidance, feelings, and intuition very closely.

Symbolism

A beautiful mer-angel floats along the top of the water. She's the only character in the suit of merpeople with wings. This symbolizes her angelic ability to care for others.

While the mer-angel is a deeply feeling person, her past experiences with love and relationships make her able to "rise above" and see the truth of a situation without getting carried away by it.

Whales are associated with psychic gifts and the ability to delve deeply into emotional connections. They're also powerful symbols for creative gifts.

In the sky, there's a break in the clouds through which a bright star shines. What is it that we're wishing for in our relationships?

Angel Number

The Queen of Water is Card 49. We're asked to be of assistance to those around us as well as ourselves. The world needs us to be at work as part of our Divine purpose. If we require help, we can ask our angels for the guidance we need.

The number 49 reduces to 4 (4 + 9 = 13, 1 + 3 = 4). The energy of the angels and the need to seek out their help is amplified.

People

The Queen of Water is an extremely nurturing, loving, and kind person. She spends a great deal of time looking after her family and friends. She places an arm around us and speaks in a soft and compassionate voice until our problems no longer seem so large. There's also no point in not telling her the absolute truth, as she's extremely intuitive and will know if we're not completely honest.

The Queen may forget to care for herself, which can make her seem tired and drained of energy. It's very important that she shield herself daily with the royal blue light of Archangel Michael so that she can remain strong and healthy.

Astrology

The Queen is Cancer tinged with Gemini. Cancer is nurturing and caring through and through. It will see to our needs whenever possible. The Gemini energy makes the Queen an incredible communicator. We are well advised to follow her guidance, especially if the topic relates to the heart.

~

King of Water

The King of Water asks us to open our hearts and show compassion to those around us. We're also asked to open our minds to new ideas and creative ways of thinking. We may be called upon to provide our time or money to charitable organizations.

When it comes to relationships with other people, the King represents those we can fully trust. His heart is golden, and he operates with the highest degree of integrity.

Symbolism

The merman King wears a large, flowing purple cape. Purple is the color of the crown chakra and indicates that he's a person of deep inner knowledge and high morals.

The passion of the angelfish shows that the King hasn't stopped evolving emotionally or spiritually and that he feels very strongly about the causes he supports and the people in his life.

The dolphin represents community—the King is quite often a leader among the people he represents.

Angel Number

The King of Water is Card 50. The 5 energy tells us that there will be changes at this time, but that we're emotionally ready for what is to come. The 0 energy is to remind us that Source is always with us.

The number 50 reduces to 5 (5 + 0), which only emphasizes the importance of the emotional evolution we're experiencing in our lives.

People

Whereas the long-term intentions of the Knight of Water are uncertain, the King of Water is the type we can trust implicitly. A very committed romantic partner, he gives of his heart and his time in equal measure.

He's also a deeply spiritual person who's willing to work hard for those who are having difficult times, including charitable organizations. He almost always has a kind word for everyone and expects others to do the same. So if we've got something unkind to say about someone, it's probably best if we say it where he won't hear us.

Astrology

It's no surprise that our King is such a wonderful person. His energy is Pisces, with Aquarius thrown in. Pisces is a very intuitive and deeply caring sign of the zodiac, and Aquarius is the humanitarian sign that feels compelled to help save humankind.

~

THE SUIT OF AIR

Ace of Air

Brilliant new ideas and inspirations. Seeing the truth of a situation. A challenging beginning.

Ace of Air

The Ace of Air can be challenging, as many people misunderstand this card. Some believe that it's a sign of being asked to give up on important endeavors. When we run into obstacles while attempting to manifest our plans, we may think, *Oh well, I guess I'm just not supposed to move forward.* And often that's true. But not with the Ace of Air. There may be bumps along the road with this card, but those minor setbacks should be looked upon as Heaven helping us. Perhaps our angels are stalling us until the perfect timing presents itself. They may be using challenges to better prepare us for what's to come, or sending us the message that we need to make some minor course corrections. But we are *not* to give up! The Ace of Air generally turns out well in time!

This card can also be a clue that we're about to have an inspired new idea or revelation that gives us a better understanding of our situation.

Symbolism

Unicorns are creatures of pure energy and positive intentions. We must maintain hope even though we're going through troublesome times.

This particular unicorn is winged to indicate that our inspired new ideas will take us to new heights.

The winged unicorn stands on a large trunk of a massive tree that looks very sturdy but is growing in a twisted and unexpected way. Our plans may not unfold as we expect, but that doesn't mean that we're not supported.

There are sprouts of new growth all around the unicorn, meaning that our ideas will take root and grow if we're patient.

Angel Number

Now we come to Card 51. The energy of change that accompanies the number 5 is now matched with the need to hold positive thoughts. As we move through the Suit of Air and the challenges it can bring, faith is what will get us happily to our goal.

The number 51 reduces to 6 (5 + 1). This is the number of worry, especially when it comes to material things. What we need will be provided if we remember to simply believe.

Astrology

Aces aren't associated with a particular astrological aspect. Instead, they're connected to the element of their suit. Therefore, the Ace represents the element of Air. It also represents the three zodiac signs of the same element: Gemini, Libra, and Aquarius.

~

Being unable or unwilling to make a decision.
A stalemate. Pretending there is no problem.

Two of Air

The Two of Air is largely a stalemate. We find ourselves unable to choose, so we don't move forward at all. Usually this card reflects an inner conflict where we're at odds with ourselves. Part of this dilemma may be that we just don't want to face the issues at hand. The decision may simply be too difficult or painful to make, so we push it to the bottom of our to-do list or pretend the problem isn't there in the hopes that it will just resolve itself. The card asks us to make a choice—to move forward. We must release ourselves from the trap of avoidance, and only *we* have the key to set us free.

This card can also indicate that we're in a war of wills with someone else. If that's the case, the card asks us to find a compromise, or seek mediation with a third party.

Symbolism

Two unicorns cross horns, indicating their inability to come to a choice or compromise.

The unicorns aren't looking at each other, but merely downward, showing that they've been unable to see "eye to eye."

The unicorns are both beautiful, but they are very different from one another: one is white, and the other is a painted unicorn of brown and white. We may find one choice more to our tastes, but it's also possible that our decision is painted by someone else's desires for us.

Stars of light sparkle around the unicorns. Stars are signs of hope, showing that it's possible to free ourselves of this challenge, but it may require a "spark" of inspiration.

Angel Number

The number 52 corresponds to the Two of Air. This number tells us that it's necessary to make the changes we're considering in order to improve our situation.

The number 52 reduces to a 7 (5 + 2) to indicate that we can get back on our path if we simply listen to our Divine guidance.

Astrology

This card is associated with Moon in Libra, which is often trying to create a perfect balance. It's adept at seeing both sides of any situation; therefore, it's possible for Libra to be torn and unable to choose. This can make Moon in Libra energy uncertain or unconfident with respect to which decision to follow.

~

Three of Air

Tarot mirrors our experiences in life, and that includes the moments that fill us with sadness. The Three of Air card shows us that there's something in our lives that needs to be healed. We may have suffered a loss, or perhaps we're still haunted by pain from the past.

The two keys to recovering from our sorrow are *time* and *forgiveness*. Some experiences just take time to heal from, and it's best if we *allow* ourselves this time. Forgiveness of ourselves or others is also an important step to finding our happiness again.

Symbolism

Two unicorns console their foal, which symbolizes that it's not only okay, but probably preferable, to seek out friends or family members to help us heal from our sadness.

The small purple flowers are called "forget-me-nots," which are known for healing trauma and allowing us to let go of guilt.

We've seen this tree trunk before in the Ace of Air card; however, there has been a great deal of growth in the greenery coming from the tree. This is to show us that we will grow from the situation we find ourselves in and become stronger.

Angel Number

The Three of Air is Card 53. The 5 energy represents a significant change in our lives, which can be difficult and sometimes sad. But in time, we grow from what we've learned. The 3 energy is to comfort us and let us know that very loving ascended masters such as Jesus are with us. The 3 can also denote that talking about what troubles us would be very beneficial.

The number 53 reduces to an 8 (5 + 3). As we go through this time of uncertainty and sadness, we can be assured that we will grow and have a more abundant life in the future.

Astrology

Saturn in Libra is the attribution for the Three of Air. The sign of Libra is ruled by Venus, the planet most closely associated with love and relationships. Saturn is the planet of restriction and often brings us challenges with its presence. Therefore, the matchup of Saturn and Libra can be associated with sadness that may occur in our personal lives.

~

Four of Air

Time to rest or take a vacation.
Allow more time before making a decision.
Meditation may provide answers.

Four of Air

The previous few cards have brought with them considerable challenges. Therefore, the Four of Air asks us to take a rest. We may be mentally, physically, or emotionally exhausted, and some time away from the challenges of daily life would be welcome. This card can also suggest that we need more time before reaching any major life decisions. A better solution may reveal itself if we simply wait a little bit longer.

This is often a card that suggests meditation. It may be for our health, or it could be that we've intellectualized a problem to the point that mental exercise will no longer help us. The answer will come from going within.

Symbolism

Four unicorns have assembled as a group. The number 4 is one of angelic assistance, but it's also one of balance. The unicorns' presence indicates that our lives need more balance, and that's why some rest would benefit us.

The sleeping unicorn is taking time to rejuvenate and get its strength back.

The other three unicorns watch over the sleeping unicorn so that it can feel safe to take time off. This signifies that we should ask others to help us find time to rest if we can't quite pull it off by ourselves.

The white flowers with the pink centers are phlox, which symbolize "sweet dreams."

Angel Number

The Four of Air resonates with the energy of 54. The need to take care of ourselves and make healthy changes is emphasized by the energy of the 5. The 4 energy reminds us that our angels can be anywhere we need them to be at any time (including protecting us while we rest).

The number 54 reduces to 9 (5 + 4). Once we've rested, we will once again be called upon by our angels to make a difference in the world.

Astrology

The astrology for this card is Jupiter in Libra, which is a very intellectual association. Libra is always thinking, always processing, always intellectualizing. Jupiter is a planet of great benevolence and good fortune, so it comes into the sign of Libra to get a rest—to allow it to stop processing long enough to get the break it truly needs.

~

An unwise choice. Learn what you can from this situation. Review everyone's motives.

Five of Air

Try as we might, we don't always make the right choices. However, since everything happens for a reason, we will surely learn many things that will help us in similar situations in the future. The Five of Air card doesn't show up in a reading to chastise us. Instead, it presents itself to give us a heads-up that we may be going in a direction that won't ultimately make us happy. Making a course correction now will save us a great deal of trouble later.

The card also lets us know that there may be others around us who have different motives than we do. Their reasons for what they're doing may or may not be questionable; they're just not in line with ours. Communication can create an environment where everyone's integrity can be confirmed.

Symbolism

Five unicorns stand around in a group, yet nothing appears to be getting done. There doesn't seem to be any communication going on. The lack of movement indicates that the unicorns aren't clear about their common goals.

The background of the image is hazy, representing our inability to see clearly.

The flowers are yellow, the hue that represents the solar-plexus chakra. We may not feel empowered at this moment in our lives due to a lack of certainty regarding our direction or others' intentions.

Angel Number

The Five of Air brings with it the lesson of the number 55. With the energy of change doubled by two 5's, we see the urgency of moving in a new direction. We must take control and make our lives what we desire them to be.

The number 55 reduces to 1 (5 + 5 = 10, 1 + 0 = 1). Our thoughts create our reality, so it's important to break away from our fears.

Astrology

Venus in Aquarius is a very independent and even rebellious energy. It may not feel the need to get input from others when making choices, preferring to "go it alone." Sometimes this works well, and other times, things can go awry. This energy is also sometimes seen as aloof by other people; a lack of communication can create misunderstandings.

$\sim$

Things are looking up! The end of a difficult situation. Taking a trip.

Six of Air

Ah, finally! We can see the end of challenging times, and now we have the chance to move on. The Six of Air represents the "light at the end of the tunnel." The stress in our shoulders falls away, and what we see before us is the light of a brand-new day. Conflicts get resolved, and those who suffer from depression find relief.

This card can mean taking a trip (especially one that requires traveling by or over water). It can also represent the beginning of a metaphorical journey in our lives.

Symbolism

A unicorn is sailing out of troubled times on its way to sunnier skies. It has made course corrections and proper choices in order to leave stagnancy behind.

The ship is *Novus,* which is Latin for "new": new opportunities, new dreams, new life.

The five unicorns from the Five of Air are in the background, showing that our sailing unicorn has left that energy behind.

Angel Number

The number for this card is 56. The energy of 6 is most often one of worry, especially about material issues such as finances. However, the 5 energy indicates that changes are in progress or already occurring that will improve the situation.

The number 56 reduces to 11 (5 + 6), a master number that doesn't reduce down further. This is a number of great manifesting ability, making it all the more important that we not focus on outcomes that aren't desirable.

Astrology

Mercury in Aquarius has the ability to think outside the box. It is the planet of mental activity, while Aquarius is known for being eclectic or even outright rebellious. The two combined create opportunities that present unique solutions to problems at lightning speed! Now, Aquarius also likes to break a rule or two, so we shouldn't be surprised if the source of the "light at the end of the tunnel" that Aquarius comes up with makes one or two people unhappy.

~

Plans that need revision. More going
on than meets the eye. Poor timing.

Seven of Air

The Seven of Air reveals itself to us as a message of kindness
from Heaven. Our angels want us to know that our current path is
probably not the one we are meant to be on. We may be unaware
of our situation or oblivious to the actions of others. This card has
a traditional meaning that encompasses something being taken
away from us, but the most common loss is our freedom. What we
don't realize is that the individual taking away our independence

is ourselves. Our lack of focus on our own needs and life purpose creates a sense of limbo where we don't get where we want to go.

This card can also signify that our plans themselves are fine, but the timing of them needs an adjustment.

Symbolism

Five unicorns spin on a merry-go-round. They ride without any ability to determine their destination.

Five is the number of change. The only way to break the cycle of the merry-go-round is to change our circumstances.

The merry-go-round operates in a counterclockwise motion. This is opposed to the idea of time marching forward—that is, being able to move ahead with our lives.

In the rear of the card, we can see that two of the unicorns have broken free. They no longer have saddles on their backs, indicating that they're now masters of their own path.

Angel Number

The Seven of Air is assigned to the number 57. This card has the 5 energy of change combined with the 7 energy of being on the right path. The Seven of Air has initiated a change in direction that will bring us a more fulfilling and happy life.

The number 57 reduces to a 3 (5 + 7 = 12, 1 + 2 = 3). To further facilitate our ability to walk away from a life that isn't working out for our Divine life purpose, we can ask for help from the ascended masters, many of whom also made such life-changing choices during their time on Earth.

Astrology

The astrological attribution for this card is Moon in Aquarius. In simple terms, the Moon reflects our needs. Aquarius is a sign with a rebellious nature, but it also has a humanitarian streak that wants to save the world. With this energy, we *need* to be free, and we *need* to make a difference. This is difficult to do when we're passive and not in control of our own path.

~

Eight of Air

*An illusion of being trapped. A lack
of self-confidence. Afraid to take action.*

Eight of Air

The Eight of Air is a card that points out our lack of self-confidence, but Heaven wishes to break through our unhealthy illusions. We have a sense that we're trapped or not in control of our own lives, but that isn't true. There's always a way to free ourselves of situations that we're not happy about, but we must believe in ourselves. We must see the truth of our situation and take action.

This card can also indicate confusion or feeling helpless.

Symbolism

A single unicorn has broken free from a herd that's clustered very close together. By stepping ahead, the single unicorn has shown confidence in itself. It doesn't need to rely on the others or be part of a "pack mentality" in order to be successful.

The seven unicorns in the background appear to be standing still, with their feet in the water near the shore. Water is a symbol of emotion, and since this card is one where our fears are getting the best of us, the unicorns are standing in their fear.

The single unicorn is moving forward in a gallop across the earth, which represents being grounded in our choices. It is also running past a mushroom, which is often a symbol of good fortune. But to get to the mushroom, the unicorn had to move out of the illusion of entrapment.

Angel Number

The number for this card is 58. The energy of the 8 tells us that our endeavors are likely to be rewarded either financially or in terms of other types of abundance—as long as we're willing to make the changes necessary (this is the 5 energy).

The number 58 reduces to 4 (5 + 8 = 13, 1 + 3 = 4), indicating that our angels can help us hear the messages we need to, with compassion for the messenger.

Astrology

Jupiter in Gemini is the attribution for the Eight of Air card. Gemini is a very brilliant sign, brimming over with ideas. Jupiter is the planet of expansion. So what do you get when you take a sign that already has more ideas than it knows what to do with and add to it the planet that multiplies everything it touches? You get an astrological aspect that's frozen and unable to operate because there are too many options to manage!

~

Nine of Air

Expecting the worst. Self-fulfilling prophecies. Sleepless nights.

Nine of Air

Have you ever heard of a self-fulfilling prophecy? It's a situation where people focus so much on their fears that they eventually manifest into reality. The Nine of Air is a card sent by our angels when we're in the process of manifesting an unhappy outcome that's simply not necessary. We should think of this card as a kind and loving note from Heaven to change the way we're thinking. We need to find a way to concentrate on the results we're hoping for rather than worrying that a bad outcome is on its way.

This card can also indicate sleeplessness or insomnia, unhappy dreams, or illness caused by stress.

Symbolism

The first thing we notice about this card is that all the unicorns are asleep except one. Eight unicorns are sleeping soundly (8 being the number of abundance and positive energy), while the one remaining unicorn appears to be on watch.

Being on watch is a practice that allows others to rest while one member of the group keeps a wary eye out for situations that could cause harm. So the awake unicorn's concern is that something unpleasant might happen.

Fireflies are a very magical symbol that has many important meanings (most of them relevant to this card). They represent illumination, or "seeing the light." If we're living an enlightened life, then we know not to focus on the negative, but to keep our thoughts positive. Fireflies shine their light out from within, just as we're asked to do as children of the Divine.

Another symbolic meaning of fireflies is that something magical is afoot! If we just have faith, then anything is possible!

A waterfall can also have multiple meanings, one of which has to do with water as a symbol of emotion. A waterfall is a very powerful downward movement of water. This symbol may be indicating someone whose emotions are focused downward instead of in a more positive upward energy.

The waterfall can also be seen as a great release of water (emotion), asking us to release our negativity in this situation.

Angel Number

The Nine of Air is Card 59. The 9 energy is one of service and duty, and indicates the importance of accomplishing our spiritual mission on Earth. The 5 shows that changes may be necessary to get us on track toward our Divine life purpose.

The number 59 reduces to 5 (5 + 9 = 14, 1 + 4 = 5). The message that change is required is reinforced by the additional 5 energy.

Astrology

Mars in Gemini can be a challenging aspect. Mars is a very aggressive planet that always wants to be in motion. Gemini is brilliant, but is also constantly thinking and communicating. This can create an energy that is actively imagining outcomes (many that are negative), and then talking about these possibilities until they manifest.

～

Ten of Air

The end of a difficult situation.
Embrace the change, and expect things to
get better now. Recovering from an addiction.

Ten of Air

In traditional tarot, this is considered a very undesirable card. And with the imagery that was historically portrayed, that's no surprise. However, much like many of the Air suit cards, we feel that this is a misinterpretation. The Ten of Air most definitely represents an ending. It's just that more often than not, it's an ending that has been anticipated and quite possibly welcomed. It's a weight off our shoulders. We may be sad about the ending, but at least it's finally over and we can move on. When we're no longer hanging on to "what has been," we can begin to create a beautiful new life of "what will be."

This card can also indicate someone who's recovering from an addiction—the emphasis being on the recovery. One other thing, though, about the Ten of Air card is that it often comes with a bit of drama tied to it. So while we may be at peace with the ending, others may have their own energy around the change.

Symbolism

Eight unicorns are on a trek deep into the forest. Their destination is unclear, and also appears to be constricted and tight due to the many trees.

Two of the unicorns have turned back. They see that the path the other unicorns are on will lead nowhere, so they've concluded that the journey is over. They'll seek out a new opportunity in the open meadow.

Two of the unicorns are headed past a mushroom, a traditional symbol of good fortune and longevity. By accepting the end of their previous quest, they open the door for Heaven to bless them with something exciting and uplifting.

Angel Number

This is Card 60. The energy of the 6 is one of the material world. Our focus on "the real world" may be blocking us from a true sense of the peace we desire. The energy of 0 is our connection with the Divine.

The number 60 reduces to 6 (6 + 0), further indicating a focus on accomplishments in the physical world.

Astrology

Sun in Gemini is attributed to the Ten of Air. Gemini is a wonderful sign relating to the gift of communication. However, sometimes it can focus on the negative side of a story that would be best left untold. The upside to this is that we may come upon certain truths that, while difficult to hear, *do* set us free. And in the long run, freedom is always better than operating without knowing the whole story.

~

Page of Air

Pages are often messages or messengers, and the Page of Air is no different. Information comes to us that can be very useful, or it may be informing us of temporary delays or changes to our plans. The message we receive may not be delivered with the soft energy we'd prefer; however, that doesn't mean it's not very useful information to have. Frankly, it's often quite brilliant! The thing to remember about this card is to separate the message from the messenger.

The Page of Air can also refer to legal documents, constructive criticism, or even just plain gossip.

Symbolism

Our beautiful Page is ready for the task at hand, with many friends as backups. The card asks us to be prepared to act on the information we receive.

She carries a sword, which symbolizes truth and justice; however, it's important to note that the sword is double-edged. The truth can be cutting if not delivered in a kind way.

The ball of golden light shows that this Page is not without her own kind of magic. She can conjure up a solution or a brilliant new idea in the blink of an eye. This indicates that we may have to use original ideas or think fast on our feet.

The symbolism of wolves is very rich; however, the two things we need to remember are that they're very intelligent and their hearing is very keen (note the ears). So listen carefully to the information you receive.

Lions symbolize courage, power, and strength (hence, their presence in the Strength card). We must have confidence in our actions and act with integrity.

Unicorns are creatures of great purity of intention. Winged ones show us that we can attain great heights by standing true to our principles.

Angel Number

The Page of Air is Card 61. She knows that her thoughts create her reality and that worry is a wasted emotion. Her focus is only on what she wishes to manifest, rather than on what she fears.

The number 61 reduces to a 7 (6 + 1), which tells us that we're on our path and that doors will open for us as we continue to move forward.

People

The Page of Air is very interested in fresh ideas, trying out new things, and anything that feeds her vast curiosity about the world. If there's an Indigo child in the tarot, she is definitely the one. The Indigos are a very special group of people born with the ability to instantly know the difference between truth and lies. And this very much defines the Page of Air.

They do sometimes speak rather bluntly. This Page doesn't mean anything personal by her lack of politeness (well, usually she doesn't). She's just not very tactful. But regardless of how it's delivered, her message is likely to be extremely valuable.

Astrology

The Pages in tarot don't represent a particular astrological attribution, but are associated with a season and a geographical area of the world. The Page of Air represents winter and the American continents.

~

Knight of Air

The Knight of Air is probably the fastest-moving energy in tarot. Our lives may seem to be moving very slowly (or even not moving at all), but when this Knight shows up, it's like stepping into a whirlwind! While all the Knights are very active cards that speak of taking action, this particular Knight thinks his way through to successful solutions. This isn't the time for making emotional choices. Decisions must be made via the intellect.

Because the movement is so swift, it can be difficult to think through our choices before acting. And yet, it's still important to ponder our alternatives and fully consider what our desired outcome is before we get too far down the road.

Symbolism

The Knight and his companion are moving very swiftly. The Knight has to hold on tight in case he's thrown off the unicorn. It's important that we see to all the necessary details lest *we* be "thrown" off our course.

The unicorn's horn is quite magical and is even lit up, which indicates the spark of brilliance coming from its mind.

Swords are symbolic of courage, justice, and even clarity of purpose. This sword is lit up to show that the Knight's quest is one of integrity.

The symbols for Capricorn and Aquarius are on the bridle of the horse to indicate the astrology of the card.

The Knight wears a red dragon on his chest, signifying the passion he feels for his endeavor.

Angel Number

The number for the Knight is 62. The 6 energy speaks of the material world, while the 2 assures us that the power of positive thinking is on our side.

The number 62 reduces to an 8 (6 + 2), which relates to abundance and financial gain.

People

The Knight of Air's middle name may well be "Lightning," because that's how fast he moves and how brilliantly he thinks. He's the traditional Knight on a quest, and he usually has everything planned out from the beginning. He's tireless in his pursuit of success, and very idealistic. The only problem is that this Knight does have the tendency to act impulsively. His instincts are usually exactly what the moment calls for, but not always. That's why when the Knight of Air rushes into our lives, it's always a good thing to at least try to get him to sit down for a moment and discuss his plans with us.

But sometimes that can be almost impossible to do.

Astrology

This card is associated with Aquarius, with a little Capricorn thrown in. Aquarius is an air sign (just like the card), and is also quite brilliant. It wants to save the world, but it can be ungrounded. The Capricorn energy brings our Knight back down to Earth so that those brilliant ideas can manifest without chaos breaking out all over.

~

Queen of Air

The Queen of Air is often referred to as the "feng shui card" of tarot, as it signifies a life free of clutter or emotional distractions (otherwise known as *drama*). This is a card of wisdom born of many life experiences—some of them uplifting, and some of them quite challenging. There's an inner peace that has been earned. We've come to know how to handle just about any situation that comes with the card, and the past experiences it represents.

This card can also represent divorced individuals as well as people who have a very dry sense of humor.

Symbolism

A beautiful and wise Queen exhibits intense focus upon the task at hand. She conjures up a magical unicorn, as her intentions are pure and crystal clear.

Our Queen is dressed in tanzanite jewels. Tanzanite has many meanings that are reflective of this card. It connects us to our spirituality and is said to enhance clairvoyance. Tanzanite is also known for its ability to promote communication and allow us to speak our truth clearly, and is an excellent stone for attaining clarity with respect to who we are and what we want to accomplish.

The Queen of Air may not have many friends, but the ones she does have, she trusts. Just a couple of close friends (as represented by the man and woman on the card) are all she needs.

The Queen is using intellectual fire to create the unicorn. Her passion comes from her mind rather than from her heart.

Angel Number

This is Card 63. The energy of the 6 is one of the material world. Our Queen is very focused on "the real world" and has a strong streak of pragmatism and perfectionism. The 3 energy guides us to ask the ascended masters for assistance, a practice that our very experienced Queen is no doubt aware of.

The number 63 reduces to a 9 (6 + 3). If we place our focus on our Divine life purpose and service to those around us, the other details will work themselves out.

People

I like to call this amazing woman "the garage-sale queen." Much like the principles of feng shui dictate, she gets rid of anything (and perhaps, more important, every *person*) that no longer serves her life purpose. When it comes to her friends, drama queens (or kings) need not apply. She has experienced nearly everything in life, and has turned any sadness or challenges from the past into strength and an amazing sense of humor that she wields like a magic wand.

This Queen can also scan a problem or a difficult situation with a glance and immediately know what to do, which makes her an amazing confidante. But it's important to remember that she tends to steer clear of those who don't take responsibility for their own lives. She will hold us accountable if we ask for her help.

Astrology

The Queen of Air is Libra with a healthy dose of Virgo thrown in. Her Libra side is intellectual and very interested in things being fair and balanced. The Virgo side wants things to be neat and organized, with everything done "just so."

~

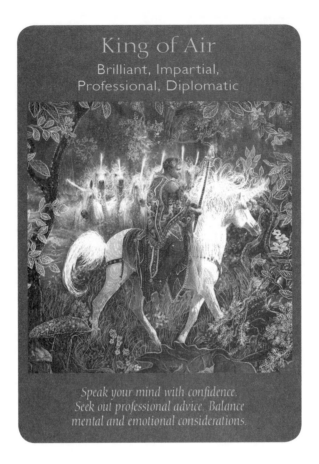

King of Air

There are times when we just need a little advice. Or perhaps someone around us needs *our* wise counsel and experience. The King of Air represents the opportunity to get the assistance we need or to help out those around us. We must feel confident to speak our truth, knowing that others will benefit from our insights. This card also reminds us that not every decision is made from the heart *or* the mind. There are times where both sources of wisdom must be balanced in order to find our way to the outcome we desire.

The King of Air can also represent the government, academia, or the military.

Symbolism

The King rides forward with confidence in his mission and in his wisdom.

He carries a spear with a light blue jewel embedded in it. The spear represents the sharpness of his mind, and the jewel is the color of the throat chakra to show that he has the ability to communicate his knowledge perfectly.

The unicorns stand at attention, anxious to hear the wisdom the King might impart.

The King rides past the mushroom, which represents good fortune. The King's abundance has already been assured by his keen mind.

Angel Number

This card is angel number 64, indicating that we're completely supported in our current undertakings. The 4 energy shows us that our angels are by our side, and the 6 energy relates to the creation of something in the material world.

The number 64 reduces to a 1 (6 + 4 = 10, 1 + 0 = 1). This is a number of immense creativity that results from our positive beliefs manifesting into reality.

People

This King is brilliant, an outstanding communicator, a perfect mediator for any dispute, and the most levelheaded person we'll ever meet. (Did I mention he's brilliant?) If we need advice about anything intellectual, career related, or logical, he has the answer, and we can rely on it fully.

The only problem is that this King is pretty much all in his head. Emotionally, he's pretty distant and not really able to connect on a heart-to-heart basis. He's fully willing to commit to a relationship; it's just that he'll operate within that romance in the same way he relates to his business partners.

Astrology

Gemini with a splash of Taurus is the astrological attribution for this card. Gemini is brilliant and able to accomplish many things at once. It's also an excellent communicator. The Taurus energy brings balance and grounding to the card so that it's not purely intellectual, but also associated with sensuality.

∼

THE SUIT OF EARTH

Ace of Earth

The inflow of abundance. A promising business venture. Important documents or contracts.

Ace of Earth

The Ace of Earth is an extremely positive card. It promises an inflow of abundance from the Universe that's often quite unexpected. While we tend to think of the word *abundance* as referring to financial prosperity, that's not always the case with this card. Our gift from Heaven may come in the form of money, or it can show up in our lives as desperately needed assistance from others, a brilliant new idea, or a person who can make introductions for us that lead to success.

This card can also indicate career advancement, a business contract, or even improved health.

Symbolism

The fairy is completely mesmerized by the gift she has received. Her ability to be so focused on her task is part of what makes her so successful.

The fairy's focal point at the top of her staff is a coin of gold, which is the icon shown throughout the suit of Earth.

The wealth of the castle in the background reminds us of the endless possibilities for "moving up the ladder" that are within our reach.

Autumn is traditionally the time of harvest. The fall colors of the plants around the fairy tell us that we can be assured that our efforts will be rewarded.

Angel Number

The Ace of Earth is Card 65, which guides us to make changes in the way we relate to money. These changes will bring us joy and abundance.

The number 65 reduces to 11 (6 + 5), which doesn't reduce further since 11 is a master number. The energy of 11 is one of powerful manifestation, as well as a spiritual concern for growth and the welfare of others.

Astrology

Aces have no specific astrological assessment, but are connected instead to the element their suit represents. This Ace represents the element of Earth. It's also associated with the three zodiac signs attributed to that element: Taurus, Virgo, and Capricorn.

~

Two of Earth

Too much going on at once. The need to make a decision. Consider a more playful approach.

Two of Earth

The Two of Earth card relates to attempting to do too much at once. That's not to say that we can't juggle our priorities and still be successful, but it may be difficult to do. Often this card indicates that someone is either working multiple jobs or hoping to move from one career to another. If we're attempting a career change, then this card would suggest that we hold off making the move until the situation (often our finances) has become more certain or secure.

This card can also be offering the advice that if we're experiencing a lot of stress or are having challenges making decisions, then a more playful approach would be beneficial.

Symbolism

A beautiful fairy is moving quickly through the forest while juggling two coins above her head. This is a difficult task and must be done carefully lest she lose her balance and drop them. This can represent attempting to do too much at once or having multiple jobs.

The rainbow in the background represents the promise that once the current storm passes, things will most definitely improve.

The daisies beneath the fairy are symbols that we need to simplify our lives by removing drama-filled situations (or people) from our world.

The tree in front of the fairy can be a symbol of either our growth or (in this case) an obstacle upon our path, depending on our focus and how we perceive the situation.

Angel Number

The angel number for this card is 66. The energy of 66 is one of great worry and concern, usually over financial matters.

The number 66 reduces to 3 (6 + 6 = 12, 1 + 2 = 3). It's a good idea to ask ascended masters like Jesus or Ganesh to help us remain positive and balanced in our lives whenever we feel we need it.

Astrology

This card resonates to Jupiter in Capricorn. Jupiter is a planet of great expansion, while Capricorn is the sign that simply wants to accomplish more and build something of significance. It's easy to see how together, Jupiter and Capricorn could easily create a workaholic whose to-do list is simply more than anyone could successfully complete.

∾

Three of Earth

The power of creativity. Recognition for very high-quality work. Be a "team player."

Three of Earth

The Three of Earth is the card of great craftsmanship. Our work is impeccable and of such high quality that we receive awards for it or are offered promotions. This is a card of immense creativity—the kind we exhibit when we're following our passions. With great practice and determination, we can sail to the top of our profession.

The Three of Earth also represents outstanding teamwork, or recognition of our contribution to a group effort.

Symbolism

Three fairies work together to create a beautiful project. Each is of a different race to emphasize the power of diversity in any group effort.

The fairies are putting the finishing touches on a mechanical butterfly. This is a remarkable accomplishment that took both creativity and precision. Since butterflies represent evolution, the image signifies that they've taken responsibility for creating their own growth through their hard work.

There are three golden coins in the wings of the butterfly, showing that all of the fairies are rewarded for their particular contributions.

The scene takes place in a green and bountiful valley. The Three of Earth shows that our efforts are being placed in fertile soil.

Angel Number

This card is number 67, which speaks to us of our success at home and at work. We've followed our guidance and have remained true to our path.

The number 67 reduces to 4 (6 + 7 = 13, 1 + 3 = 4). We're called upon to ask our angels for assistance whenever we feel the need.

Astrology

The Three of Earth is associated with Mars in Capricorn. Mars is a fiery energy that wants to accomplish great things. Capricorn is a sign that's also focused on doing a good job and is often concerned with the legacy it may leave behind. This pairing fits perfectly with this card's emphasis on unparalleled creative work.

~

Four of Earth

*Being too frivolous or too cautious
with money. Good business decisions.
Giving to those less fortunate.*

Four of Earth

As I've mentioned, there are cards in tarot that refer to the extremes of either side of a concept. I call them duality cards. The message isn't gray, but rather, black or white. The answer isn't "maybe," but "yes" or "no." The Four of Earth tells us that we're either spending entirely too much money, or we're being so cautious with it that we're missing out on the happiness it could bring us. Which of these messages pertains to the reading is a matter of both our intuition and the other cards in the spread.

Another meaning of this card can be that we need to be more charitable with our abundance, which fits in with the extreme of hoarding our cash.

The Four of Earth sometimes refers to other situations where we are either being excessive or insufficient in our efforts. For example, we could be loving too much or not enough. We could be trying too hard or not trying at all. This card can also mean well-thought-out business decisions, large purchases or investments, or a feeling of paranoia that our prosperity will be taken from us.

Symbolism

The two fairies in the image represent the extremes noted in the card. One fairy is quite large, and the other is very small. One is completely visible, and the other is partially hidden.

One way to allow our intuition to help us know which extreme the card is referring to is to note which fairy our eyes are drawn to. The small fairy can indicate someone of small means, the larger fairy someone who has a much larger accumulation of assets.

We can also note that the basket of coins is chained to the larger fairy, indicating that she's the one who should let go of her tight hold upon her wealth in order to help those in need.

The smaller fairy doesn't even have a "shirt on her back," showing that she may be lacking in resources.

Angel Number

The number 68 is connected with the Four of Earth card. We're inspired to know that Spirit is the source of our abundance and that prayer can work miracles.

The number 68 reduces to 5 (6 + 8 = 14, 1 + 4 = 5). This is the number that tells us that changes are coming in our lives; we just need to be patient.

Astrology

Sun in Capricorn is the astrological association for this card. The sign of Capricorn is one of dedication and concentration on its task. However, we must remember that Capricorn is ruled by Saturn, the planet of restriction. This can create the paradox we see in the Four of Earth. The Capricorn Sun is always there, wanting to shine for work well done, while the energy of Saturn may hold us back from enjoying the fruits of our labors.

∿

Five of Earth

Fears surrounding money. The wisdom to accept help from others. Uncertain self-employment.

Five of Earth

The Five of Earth tells us that something is lacking in our lives. This situation may be real, but it's more often a perception that the card is asking us to change. While the card is oriented toward financial worries, we believe that it can also represent an absence of friends, romance, or opportunities. Of course, as long as our focus is on that which we don't have, the Law of Attraction will only bring us more of the experience of lack. The Five of Earth indicates that there's help at hand, but we may be too distracted or too proud to ask for it.

This card is a temporary situation that eventually fades away once our thoughts turn to a more positive energy. It can also reflect a situation where a change in career—especially a transition to self-employment—would be unwise at this time.

Symbolism

The path before us is tangled and overgrown. It would appear that getting to our destination is going to be difficult, if not impossible.

However, a cuckoo bird flies over a narrow path that leads to a beautiful tower. The cuckoo is a symbol of a change in our circumstances, but it is within us to change that situation if we so desire.

The path leads to a beautiful tower lit by five golden coins. There's help waiting there for us if we will just ask for it.

Five is the number of change, and the rationale for the five golden coins on the tower.

Angel Number

The Five of Earth resonates to the number 69. The 9 energy speaks of those who may be experiencing a sense of emptiness due to being off their Divine path. The 6 energy is one of worry over material or financial concerns.

The number 69 reduces to 6 (6 + 9 = 15, 1 + 5 = 6), emphasizing the importance of being paid a fair wage for our efforts.

Astrology

Mercury in Taurus isn't inclined to move quickly. While Mercury is a sign that's capable of zooming right along, the grounding side of Taurus can bring things to a standstill. When this energy has its mind set on something, it can be difficult to get it to change. There's a desire to do things on its own that can prevent it from asking for help or moving along the path—even when doing so could make the situation much better.

～

Gifts of money, time, or effort. New career opportunities. Receiving a loan or paying off debts.

Six of Earth

The challenges of the Five of Earth have fallen away, and what's left is the abundance and generosity inherent in the Six of Earth. Prosperity enters our lives in the form of gifts or increases in salary due to our outstanding work. The power of positive thinking has brought us to a new time of abundance. This card can also reflect paying off debts, the repayment of favors, or the elimination of other obligations.

The Six of Earth is a card of gratitude and charity. By giving thanks to the Universe for what we have, more is provided to us. We're called upon to give our time, energy, or financial gifts to others who are less fortunate.

Symbolism

The fairy in this image was previously seen working with others to create the work of art in the Three of Earth. His hard work has brought him to a place of prosperity.

The scales are currently unbalanced, reflecting a society where not everyone has all that they need. The fairy who has found that abundance in his life works to restore balance by enabling him to give to those in need.

Angel Number

This is Card 70, which signifies good work that has flourished, and also those who are on the right path.

The number 70 reduces to 7 (7 + 0), which merely intensifies the message of success.

Astrology

The energy around Moon in Taurus is thoughtful, kind, and giving. It is very connected to that which matters in life, with a full understanding of the truth. The way this energy sees things may not be the same way others do, but it is dedicated to its convictions.

$\sim$

Seeds well planted. A temporary
pause in action. Unnecessary worry.

Seven of Earth

The Seven of Earth is a card of hope, and also patience. Our efforts will be rewarded, but like seeds planted in a garden, it will take time for our work to bear fruit. Often when this card is drawn, someone is fearful that desired results will not pan out. However, the Seven of Earth represents worry that's unfounded. All will be well in time.

If it feels as though events have come to a standstill, it's only temporary. Soon our plans will begin to gain momentum again.

Symbolism

A living tree in an enchanted forest has grown, and now blossoms with gold coins. Trees take time to reach maturity and bloom, the same as our current endeavor.

The tree sprouts seven gold coins. Seven is the number that assures us that we're on the correct path.

A fairy visits the tree, wishing to have a conversation. Fairies are magical beings who are known as powerful manifesters.

Angel Number

This is Card 71, a number that tells us that our lives are right on track and that the dreams we've chosen to manifest are coming true. We simply need to stay positive in our thoughts to continue to prosper.

The number 71 reduces to 8 (7 + 1), which is the number of abundance and financial security.

Astrology

Saturn in Taurus is the astrological association for this card. Taurus is a sign that very much enjoys luxury and comfort, but Saturn is a planet that holds us back from immediately getting what we want. We learn from Saturn in order to grow and eventually attain our goals—although our growth may change our minds about what it is we're hoping for.

∼

Skilled work is rewarded. Learning all there is to know about a topic. Going back to school.

Eight of Earth

If the Three of Earth is the great master craftsman, then the Eight of Earth is the apprentice. With this card, we throw ourselves into our studies until we know all there is to know, and practice our vocation until our skills are honed. We work extremely hard on our current project until every aspect has been attended to. Our eyes are set on perfection, and we're determined to make the grade.

This card can also refer to going back to school, attending a seminar, or taking an online class—anything that has to do with educating ourselves or further developing our skills.

Symbolism

A young male fairy sits in a field studying. The greenery around him is lush, but very little is blooming. He still has much to learn before his skills blossom and flower.

The fairy wears a crown, indicating that he may be a prince, but this fact doesn't sway him from learning a trade. This card represents people who are diligent and conscientious.

There are eight books for our fairy to read. Eight is the number of abundance, indicating that he wishes to make a prosperous living from his studies.

The fairy attends to his lessons in seclusion—away from friends, family, or other distractions that might keep him from gleaning all there is to know about the topic he's studying.

Angel Number

The Eight of Earth is Card 72. The 2 energy tells us that our research will inspire us to lead the life we so want to live. The 7 energy tells us to have faith, as we are on the perfect path to achieve what we desire!

The number 72 reduces to a 9 (7 + 2), telling us that our efforts are carrying us toward our Divine life purpose.

Astrology

Sun in Virgo is the astrological designation for this card. Virgos are known for being extremely exacting in their work, with a focus on minute details. Those born under the sign of Virgo are individuals of service who care very much about other people's welfare.

$\sim$

Enjoying life's little luxuries. Spending quiet time alone. Successful self-employment.

Nine of Earth

The Nine of Earth is a card of success, luxury, and self-nurturing. Our prosperity hasn't been handed to us, but earned by many hours of long, hard work. We deserve the rest and relaxation that we're currently experiencing. This card often refers to people nearing retirement or, at the very least, those who've earned enough money to stop working if they so choose. This card is a sign that plans to go into business for ourselves are well founded and should be pursued.

This is also a card of quiet reflection. We've learned the difference between pleasant solitude and being lonely. We enjoy our time in nature and don't need the company of others to be happy.

Symbolism

A female fairy walks quietly through a beautiful scene in nature. She planted this garden, and the maturity of the trees and flowers indicate that she's been very patient and diligent in tending to the surroundings.

The fairy's beautiful dress and crown indicate that she's a person of wealth.

This fairy was previously seen working on the mechanical butterfly in the Three of Earth. She has arrived at this moment in her life through hard work, creativity, and seeing to all the details.

The flowers are clematis, which are known to symbolize ingenuity. And like our fairy, these flowers are quite adept at attaining new heights in life.

Angel Number

This card is number 73, symbolizing good work that has flourished, and those who are on the right path. The ascended masters have helped us reach our goals!

The number 73 reduces to 1 (7 + 3 = 10, 1 + 0 = 1), which speaks to our ability to manifest whatever we want at the present time.

Astrology

Venus in Virgo is in pursuit of grounded, beautiful perfection. It enjoys a simple life as long as everything is in its place. This is a very down-to-earth energy that values its privacy and time alone.

～

Ten of Earth

A very happy family life. Financial security. Finding magic in the little things in life.

Ten of Earth

The Ten of Earth is a card of financial security and joyful contentment. There's a strong concern for family; however, the focus is more on aspects such as family lineage, knowing that the children's futures are financially secure, and material comforts. Home and hearth are very important. The Ten of Earth is one of the cards in tarot where everything just feels right, and we've earned the right to be very proud of ourselves.

This card can also reflect communities that we feel very connected to, inheritance, and successful completion. The card may relate to gay relationships or a family with same-sex partners.

Symbolism

A beautiful family has gathered in a forest setting. Everyone is smiling, and there's a sense of contentment.

The children are happily playing with golden coins, which represent that their futures are financially secure. It can also indicate an inheritance.

The family is of a nontraditional nature to symbolize that the word *family* means many different things to different people. It may represent the family we were born to, a family of friends who support one another, or a community of individuals who have mutual goals.

Fireflies represent the magic in life . . . and with the Ten of Earth, life *is* magical.

Angel Number

This is Card 74; it tells us that our lives are right on track and that the dreams we've chosen to manifest are coming true. We're reminded to express gratitude to the angels for all their assistance.

The number 74 reduces to 11 (7 + 4), which is a master number and does not reduce further. This magical number tells us that we've used our ability to manifest to create deeply moving experiences.

Astrology

Mercury in Virgo is very good at "taking care of business." It has every detail figured out and is extremely good at communicating its wishes. Intellectually, its sheer brilliance can also be quite creative.

~

Page of Earth

If you're looking for a little good news, you've come to the right card. The Page of Earth tends to bring us very positive information about our finances or career plans. We may find ourselves suddenly fascinated by an entirely new subject, or we may want to go back to school or just study a new topic at great length.

However, sometimes the Page of Earth indicates a sense of restlessness. We may be eager to do something more meaningful or challenging in our lives.

Symbolism

A beautiful fairy sits in a nighttime forest holding a golden coin in her right hand.

There are stars in the sky and also in her wings, which we can make wishes upon. The good news we've received will allow us to follow our dreams.

Blue butterflies are traditional symbols of joy and happiness.

The autumn-colored flowers present to us that it is a time of being rewarded for our efforts.

Angel Number

The Page of Earth is Card 75. The 5 energy tells us that there will be changes to be made due to the information we receive. Those changes will put us on just the right life path.

The number 75 reduces to a 3 ($7 + 5 = 12$, $1 + 2 = 3$), which is perfect for a messenger since the number 3 carries with it the process of communication. The ascended masters can help us carry our dreams forward.

People

The Page of Earth is the kind of kid any parent would be thrilled to have. She's clever, optimistic, wiser than her years, and oh so happy to help out! She's very interested in learning, and will research any topic through and through.

But this can be her one downfall. She loves to study so much that she might never stop reading and get to work. So we may have to wrestle those books out of her hands (if we can) and give her a gentle nudge to take action.

Astrology

The Pages in tarot don't represent a particular astrological attribution, but are associated with a season and a geographical area of the world. The Page of Earth represents autumn and the continents of Europe and Africa.

~

Time to buckle down and get things done!
Honor your commitments. A guardian angel.

Knight of Earth

The Knight of Earth tells us that it's time to move along. The planning stage is complete, and now it's time to take action! The plans we've made are excellent and will work out very well. We're encouraged to maintain our integrity throughout the process and to follow through on any promises we've made.

This card can also refer to business travel, financial rewards, and guardian angels.

Symbolism

The Knight is standing still on a horse. When we're riding a horse, we're supposed to be moving, so this reminds us to get going!

This Knight has no sword drawn, unlike the other knights. One of the things that swords represent is intellectual energy. This Knight's thinking has already been completed.

This is the only character in the Suit of Earth without fairy wings. This is because he represents a protector to the fairies in the world of humans. He is an "incarnated fairy" looking out for their well-being.

The Knight's shield is put away since his plan is so perfect that there will be nothing to defend against.

The Knight of Earth has a very fancy horse—a nod to his astrological attribution of Taurus, a sign that loves beautiful things.

Angel Number

The angel number for this card is 76. We know that our financial needs are met and that we're on the path for our Divine life purpose.

The number 76 reduces to 4 (7 + 6 = 13, 1 + 3 = 4). Since the number 4 relates to angels, it's perfect for a card that itself represents a guardian angel.

People

While the Knight of Earth doesn't move all that quickly, his plans are perfect. No matter what needs to be done, he can figure out how to get it successfully completed with at least three back-up plans.

He's charming, gallant, honorable, and completely trustworthy. He loves nature (hence, his role as the protector of the fairies), and is usually a vegetarian or a vegan. Anyone who hurts an animal is likely to get on his bad side. Just because he's put his sword away doesn't mean he can't get it out if he feels the need.

Astrology

Our Knight is Taurus with a healthy measure of Aries thrown in. Taurus is known for its love of beauty and luxurious items. Very sensual in nature, it can also be quite stubborn. If it doesn't want to move, then good luck getting it going. That's where Aries comes in. Once Taurus is ready to go, the Aries part of this Knight can accomplish a great deal!

~

Queen of Earth
Thoughtful, Creative,
Warm, Sensible

Make time for those around you.
Take a sensible approach. Deal with challenges
in a kind and understanding manner.

Queen of Earth

There's a lot of magic going on in the Queen of Earth card. Golden coins are flying everywhere, showing that we're in a time of manifestation. We have just about everything figured out, and we prefer taking a very down-to-earth approach to our problems. However, we're also being called upon to make sure that those around us are getting their needs met. We can't forget our families and friends just because our careers are busy.

This card is also a reminder to use kindness in our interactions with others. We may think we understand their situations, but it's quite possible that they're going through more than we know.

Symbolism

Our Queen is an incredible manifester! In this situation, it appears to be financial in nature, but she can also make things happen in her emotional and family life.

Her magic is sending coins flying everywhere! In fact, all those coins have her likeness on them. They're also the coins we've seen in all the other cards of this suit.

The pot of gold shows that the Queen is always prepared and has abundance saved up for rainy days.

There are two bunnies at the Queen's feet. Rabbits represent fertility, abundance, and the ability to make great strides.

Angel Number

The number for our Queen is 77. The 7 energy relates to great success and a call to continue the path we're on—a very successful number!

The number 77 reduces to 5 (7 + 7 = 14, 1 + 4 = 5). The Queen of Earth is an excellent person to ask for assistance with our plans if we're feeling uncertain.

People

This Queen is an amazing friend, mother, and spouse. She can simultaneously run a company, raise money for her favorite charity, and still have time to tend her garden. She is generous to a fault and will help anyone who requires assistance.

Her one challenge may relate to money. Yes, she can conjure up golden coins from thin air and is probably very well-off financially. It's just that she also loves to *spend* that money on beautiful and luxurious things.

Astrology

The Queen of Earth is Capricorn with Sagittarius. Capricorns are often thought of as the hardest-working signs in the zodiac. This energy is one of financial prosperity and solid business sense. Sagittarius is a sign of great spiritual understanding and optimism. Capricorn makes money, but Sagittarius loves to spend it!

~

King of Earth
Generous, Professional,
Responsible, Practical

A successful time. Confidently accept
opportunities you're offered. The Midas touch.

King of Earth

The King of Earth heralds a time of incredible prosperity and success. When we draw this card, we can be assured that our plans are going to go exceptionally well. Money may appear to fall from the sky, but really it's our own hard work that has brought us to this time of abundance. This card can indicate an upcoming raise or promotion.

The King of Earth will also advise us that we should accept opportunities that come our way even if at first glance it seems as if we should turn them down.

Symbolism

The rainbow in the sky speaks of good luck, abundance, and epiphany.

The blue butterfly that signifies joy and happiness has returned. We previously saw it fluttering with the Page of Earth. The good news we got from the Page has indeed turned out to be true.

Behind the King there are stairs that lead up into the mountain. The steps to success are right there, ready to be ascended!

Dragonflies are symbols of magic. The card tells us that things will go so easily that it will *seem* like magic.

Angel Number

The number of our King is 78; this card pats us on the back for doing a wonderful job, and at the same time fills our coffers with golden coins!

The number 78 reduces to 6 (7 + 8 = 15, 1 + 5 = 6), which resonates to the energy of concerns over material comforts.

People

The King of Earth has the Midas touch. Everything he comes into contact with turns to gold, but that's not the extent of his concerns. He cares very much for people and is often an excellent manager. Like the Queen of Earth, he feels the need to take care of others. In his case, this is more likely to be in the form of donations to charities and helping all sorts of people when necessary. The King is a dedicated environmentalist.

Also, he is often a workaholic, so he may not be home as much as we'd like.

Astrology

The King is largely Virgo but has a Leo side to him. Virgo is known for being a very hardworking sign that lives to serve. And this King fits that bill. However, just like Leo, this King does like a bit of the spotlight and definitely wants to be recognized for his good work—preferably in front of a large group of people.

ABOUT *the* ARTIST

You can order prints of many of the images in the *Angel Tarot Cards* deck. The prints come in different sizes without the border or words that appear on the cards. To purchase a print, please contact the artist directly through the methods listed below. Neither Hay House, Inc.; Magical Things, Inc.; nor Radleigh Valentine assumes responsibility for any sales conducted between you and the artist.

All Artwork by Steve A. Roberts

An artist of vision and technique, **Steve A. Roberts** was self-taught. This he did by studying the works of his childhood heroes—legendary fantasy artists such as Frank Frazetta and the Brothers Hildebrandt. Steve received his only formal training when he sat in on classes at the Ringling School of Art.

Born in central Florida in a little town called Palmetto, a stone's throw from the Gulf of Mexico, he began drawing, like most artists, as a young child. Later, he spent 12 years in Alaska, a place that had always stirred in his imagination. In that time, Steve drove a taxi in Anchorage, worked construction, built a log cabin on 40 acres, and painted the wonders of this fairy-tale land. Meanwhile, his work was receiving more and more attention. Returning to Florida, Steve started his company, Fantasy Graphics. He was recognized as one of the most talented artists in fantasy illustration.

Website: https://steve-roberts.pixels.com/art

ABOUT *the* AUTHOR

Best-selling Hay House author **Radleigh Valentine** has inspired audiences worldwide with the angelic messages of pure love and unconditional support. He is the author of multiple angel card decks, including the best-selling *Angel Tarot Cards*. His books *How to Be Your Own Genie* and *Compendium of Magical Things* offer insightful, exhilarating lessons about how to manifest the life of our dreams and find our own unique language for communicating with the Divine.

An internationally known spiritual teacher and speaker, Radleigh has appeared at the Angel World Summit in London, Engelkongress in Germany and Austria, and more than a dozen Hay House I Can Do It events. In his weekly Hay House Radio show, *Magical Things with Radleigh Valentine*, and in the popular streaming video show, *Ask Rad!* on Facebook and Instagram, he infectiously enchants audiences with the message that each and every one of our lives . . . is magic!

For more information, please visit www.radleighvalentine.com.

Hay House Titles of Related Interest

We hope you enjoyed this Hay House book. If you'd like to receive our online catalog featuring additional information on Hay House books and products, or if you'd like to find out more about the Hay Foundation, please contact:

Hay House, Inc., P.O. Box 5100, Carlsbad, CA 92018-5100
(760) 431-7695 or (800) 654-5126
(760) 431-6948 (fax) or (800) 650-5115 (fax)
www.hayhouse.com® • www.hayfoundation.org

———

Published in Australia by: Hay House Australia Pty. Ltd.,
18/36 Ralph St., Alexandria NSW 2015
Phone: 612-9669-4299 • *Fax:* 612-9669-4144
www.hayhouse.com.au

Published in the United Kingdom by: Hay House UK, Ltd.,
The Sixth Floor, Watson House, 54 Baker Street, London W1U 7BU
Phone: +44 (0)20 3927 7290 • *Fax:* +44 (0)20 3927 7291
www.hayhouse.co.uk

Published in India by: Hay House Publishers India,
Muskaan Complex, Plot No. 3, B-2, Vasant Kunj, New Delhi 110 070
Phone: 91-11-4176-1620 • *Fax:* 91-11-4176-1630
www.hayhouse.co.in

———

**Access New Knowledge.
Anytime. Anywhere.**

Learn and evolve at your own pace
with the world's leading experts.

www.hayhouseU.com